D0045349

THE CHRIST | of the Earliest Christians

THE CHRIST of the Earliest Christians

by William M. Ramsay

JOHN KNOX PRESS
Richmond, Virginia

The Library of Congress has catalogued this book as follows:

Ramsay, William M

The Christ of the earliest Christians. Richmond, John Knox Press [1959]

156 p. 21 cm.

The author's thesis put into shorter and more popular form.
Includes bibliography.

1. Jesus Christ—Person and offices. I. Title.

BT201.R28 1959 232 59-5093 ‡

Library of Congress

Except where otherwise indicated, Scripture quotations are from the Revised Standard Version, copyright 1946 and 1952 by the Division of Christian Education of the National Council of the Churches of Christ in the United States of America. In some cases the author has italicized words or phrases for added emphasis.

Printed in the United States of America
6029

Foreword

IF JESUS OF NAZARETH is simply another martyr gone to death, then clearly the Gospel story has no unique or ultimate significance for this confused, bewildered generation, and no permanent validity for any of us seeking to adjust our lives to the demands of our strange contemporary world. But if Jesus is what the men of the New Testament declare, then—*sursum corda!*—the whole situation is utterly transformed; for we can be sure that God will not allow the world for which He gave His Son to slip through His fingers at the last.

Hence the supreme importance of the ancient question, "What think ye of Christ?"

But were the early preachers right? Some Bible students would have us believe that the high Christology of St. Paul and St. John was arbitrarily superimposed upon the simple humanitarian message of the Galilean prophet; and this view still finds numerous adherents inside the churches and out. But it ought to be known that the best scholarship has emphatically repudiated it. When Christian theology is traced back behind the canonical Gospels into the period of the underlying, primitive documentary sources, and beyond that into the oral tradition, it is discovered that no heightening of Christology took place with the passing of the years, for the highest possible Christology is there from the first. In fact, it can be said with assurance that it derives ultimately from Jesus Himself.

This, then, is the importance of the study which Dr. Ramsay here presents. The Christian religion does not begin at Bethlehem; it begins at the throne of God. The true dimension of our holy faith is the eternal mystery that expressed itself once for all in those quiet, shattering words of the Johannine Christ: "Before Abraham was, I am." What we Christians worship is not a human life that climbed up to God by a process of deification—it is God coming down into humanity by an act of incarnation, an event of a totally different quality. We shall never begin to understand Christianity, never realize why the Church of the early centuries was able to hit the Roman Empire like a thunderbolt, until we have set Bethlehem and Calvary against their proper background—which is this background of eternity, this thrust and pressure of the supernatural. And if anyone should imagine that all this is remote, irrelevant theology, the answer must be that that is precisely what it is not. Indeed, it is the one faith which is realistic enough, down-to-earth enough, to make an impact either on the Roman Empire in the first century or on the miseries and hopes of the world in the twentieth.

Do let us be clear that what as Christians we celebrate is not a human genius who went about continually doing good, teaching wonderful lessons on the Fatherhood of God and the brotherhood of man, and holding views on ethics and international politics far in advance of His time. That would never have crashed into the throne of Caesar and routed the darkness of the world. That is a poor, insipid imitation of the dynamic and explosive thing the New Testament is talking about. What the New Testament bears witness to on every page, what carried the message like a prairie fire across the world, was no such dwarfed and timid version of the Gospel. It was the astounding fact that in Jesus of Nazareth the ultimate and eternal had struck down into history and broken through into the life of men.

Difficult to grasp? Of course it is. Men have stumbled and stammered before the glory of it for nineteen hundred years. But how much better surely to hold this flaming, magnificent truth—which is *the* central truth of the New Testament—to hold it by a robust and daring faith, than to potter about with timid, desupernaturalized versions of it which have not dynamic enough to save a single soul, much less be the propitiation for the sins of the whole world!

This is the contemporary importance of the question, "What think ye of Christ?" And this is why it is so vital, not only that we hear the answer of the earliest heralds of the faith, but that we be able to make that answer our own.

Dr. Ramsay, having written an academic dissertation on this matter, has now put the substance of his thesis into shorter and more popular form. The pages that follow, dealing with one of the most important aspects of Christian origins, have a very relevent and compelling message for today. I commend this book to ministers and laymen alike. It deserves to be widely read and pondered.

JAMES S. STEWART

New College
The University
Edinburgh

Dedicated to

DR. AND MRS. CHARLES S. RAMSAY

my father and mother

Contents

Acknowledgments

THE AUTHOR WISHES TO THANK the many who have helped to make this book possible. A special word of appreciation is expressed to the faculty and library staff of Union Theological Seminary in Virginia; to Professor James Stewart and the late Professor William Manson of Edinburgh, under whom the research for the book was done; to the author's brother, Professor Charles M. Ramsay, Austin College, for many valuable criticisms and suggestions; to Mrs. Robert Harris and Mrs. Roger Joiner of the Forest Hills congregation, Paducah, Kentucky, for assistance in the preparation of the manuscript; and to the author's wife, DeVere M. Ramsay, for help in countless ways.

CHAPTER 1

THE CHRIST | of the Earliest Christians

"WHAT DO YOU THINK OF THE CHRIST?"

No thinking Christian can ignore this question. It is Jesus Himself who asks it. (Matthew 22:42.) Matthew describes how Jesus' enemies tried to trap Him as they challenged Him with disputes about taxes to Caesar and about a woman in heaven who had had seven husbands on earth. Jesus quickly disposed of these petty debates and turned to the subject which He knew really matters: "What do you think of the Christ?"

Who and what is Jesus? How may we put His meaning into words? What do we think of Him? For two thousand years the greatest Christian theologians have wrestled with this as the central problem of religious thought.

To guide us in our own response to Jesus, nothing could be of more importance than the first ideas about Him, the things that were said of Him by those who first experienced His resurrection and the coming of His Spirit. *What did the very first Christians think of Jesus?*

We know the doctrine of Christ propounded by the ancient church in the resounding phrases of the Nicene Creed:

> I believe . . . in one Lord Jesus Christ, the only-begotten Son of God, begotten of His Father before all worlds; God of God; Light of Light; Very God of Very God; Begotten, not made; Being of one substance with the Father, by whom all things were made; Who for us men, and for our salvation, came down from heaven; And was incarnate by

> the Holy Ghost of the Virgin Mary, and was made man; And was crucified also for us under Pontius Pilate. He suffered and was buried; And the third day He rose again according to the Scriptures; And ascended into heaven; And sitteth on the right hand of the Father. And He shall come again with glory to judge both the quick and the dead; Whose kingdom shall have no end . . .[1]

But suppose a modern investigator, beset with doubts, were to examine that creed. Straightway he would notice that, however true they may be, there are phrases here never found in the New Testament. "Very God of Very God . . . of one substance with the Father . . ."—this is the language of three hundred years after Jesus. How would those who knew Him as a man have described their Lord?

Historical research can never fully answer the question, Who and what is Jesus? But research can take us back to answers nearer Jesus' earthly lifetime.

New Testament Pictures of Jesus

For Protestant Christianity the New Testament has been the great answer. But how varied are the pictures of Jesus found there!

Turning to the book of Revelation an investigator would find this description of Him:

> one like a son of man, clothed with a long robe and with a golden girdle round his breast; his head and his hair were white as white wool, white as snow; his eyes were like a flame of fire, his feet were like burnished bronze . . . ; in his right hand he held seven stars . . . (Revelation 1:13-16.)

There have been scholars who argued forcefully that this was the very earliest view of Jesus. The saintly and scholarly Albert Schweitzer,[2] along with others, has maintained that the first Christians—even Jesus Himself—thought primarily in terms of the heavenly Son of man who would come with angels to be the final Judge of all the world.

In the book of Hebrews the investigator would find Jesus described in different terms, derived from the Jewish Scriptures:

> . . . such a high priest, holy, blameless, unstained, separated from sinners, exalted above the heavens . . . a minister in the sanctuary and the true tent . . . (Hebrews 7:26; 8:2.)

Perhaps the first Christians, all of whom were Jews, thought of Jesus primarily in terms derived, like those of the Epistle to the Hebrews, from the Jewish Scriptures—particularly as the "Messiah" or "Anointed One" promised in the Old Testament.

An inquirer, asking what the first Christians thought about Jesus, would easily find out what the writers of the first three Gospels believed. Jesus is, for Mark and the others, "Christ, the Son of God" (Mark 1:1),[3] but the Gospels develop, far more than do the Revelation or the Epistle to the Hebrews, the idea of Jesus as a man among men, born in a barn and crucified on a Roman cross.

Some Bible students have thought they found in this emphasis on Jesus' earthly life a hint of the earliest idea about Him. In the beginning, they say, Jesus' followers remembered Him as a good man, but the church made a god out of Him. Paul is sometimes said to be the author of this "new" idea.[4]

Turning to the letters of Paul we find this statement, written only about twenty-five years after Jesus' death:

> . . . who was descended from David according to the flesh and designated Son of God in power according to the Spirit of holiness by his resurrection from the dead . . . (Romans 1:3-4.)

Some have believed that this and similar passages point to the earliest doctrine of the person of Christ. Jesus was a man, the son of David. But with the resurrection visions, God announced to the disciples something new. Jesus had been adopted as the Son of God.[5] God had "highly exalted him," much as the Greek hero Hercules was taken to heaven and made a god at his death. David's son had now been raised to the right hand of God as David's Lord.

The Fourth Gospel gives yet another and quite different picture of Jesus. In the Gospel of John, Jesus says:

> I am the vine. (John 15:5.)
> I am the light of the world. (John 8:12.)
> I am the way, and the truth, and the life. (John 14:6.)

Here Jesus is a living and present Power, one with whom His followers have mystic union. The experience of Pentecost may have made the disciples first recall words like these.

Can we take any of these pictures as the very first portrait of Jesus? No, the fact is that the earliest of our New Testament books was written at least twenty years after the earthly life of Jesus, and most of the New Testament was written thirty or forty years afterward. Our investigator, seeking to go further back, finds himself facing what has been called a dark "tunnel." [6] At one end of the tunnel is the historical fact of the crucifixion of Jesus. At the other end we emerge into the clear light of the New Testament. But what was said and thought about Jesus in the critical years between?

All the investigator's work must be done from this end of the tunnel. Jesus Himself wrote nothing. No contemporary of His ever attempted any strictly "objective" account of His personality. However accurate they may be historically, the Gospels are themselves interpretations of Jesus, written "from faith to faith," by Christians and for Christians. Behind the witness of the early church, research can go only by inference.

The Claims of Acts

Is it possible to get behind the time of the New Testament writings?

There were preachers who "turned the world upside down" before a word of the book was written. What of these first preachers? What did they say about Jesus?—that He was a good man? a great teacher? God of gods? something between God and man? Is there any source that can give us the very earliest answer to the most important question in Christian thought, "What do you think of the Christ?"

There is one ancient document that claims to do this very thing—one ancient book, claiming for itself a certain historical accuracy, which purports to give the earliest interpretations of Jesus. It even claims to summarize the picture of Christ preached on the Day of Pentecost, only fifty days after the crucifixion! This book is the Acts of the Apostles.

Acts 2 contains a report of the first Christian sermon ever preached. Other addresses by Peter, at least in condensed form, are recorded in Acts 3:12-26; 4:8-12; 5:29-32; and 10:34-43. Acts 7 gives the long discourse by Stephen, the first Christian martyr. And Acts 13 includes the first recorded address of the Apostle Paul.

But a sceptical investigator will straightway raise two questions. Can the account in Acts be trusted? The book itself was written perhaps fifty years after the events it claims to record. No one imagines that Peter had a stenographer present taking down his words in shorthand on the Day of Pentecost. Granted that Acts is inspired and inspiring, can it answer our historical question about the earliest witness to

Jesus? To what extent does this book, written years later, really picture the Christ of the earliest Christians?

When that question has been answered satisfactorily, another will remain. What was the original meaning of the phrases used to describe Jesus? What did the first preachers mean when they called Jesus "Christ," "Son of God," "Lord," "Servant of God"?

In Search of an Answer

Here, then, is our plan. We shall first examine, as critically as a detective, the early chapters of Acts. When we have satisfied our minds as best we can concerning the historical accuracy of this report of the first preaching, we shall examine the sermons in the first thirteen chapters of Acts to see what they tell us about the earliest ideas concerning Jesus.

It is a thrilling adventure we are beginning. It may be that we are turning to the primary historical source for an answer to the primary question of the Christian life.

CHAPTER 2

ACTS and the Earliest Answer

HOW ACCURATE, HISTORICALLY, is the book of Acts in its report of the first Christian preaching? It was written at least thirty-five and perhaps fifty years or more after Peter's sermon at Pentecost. Can we believe its account of the earliest Christian thought?

Authorship

Most students of Acts believe that it is the work of Luke, a companion of Paul and the author of the third Gospel.

That Paul's friend Luke wrote Acts is a consistent and early tradition.[1] The early church fathers disputed the authorship of several other New Testament books, but all who discuss the matter agree concerning Acts. Luke was not otherwise a very prominent figure either in the New Testament itself or in the tradition of the early church. There seems to be no reason, therefore, why the third Gospel and Acts should have been ascribed to him unless they were indeed from his pen.

Turning to Acts itself we find that its opening verses, like those of the third Gospel, are written in the first person and are addressed to one Theophilus. They refer to a first book in which the author has described the deeds of Jesus from the beginning to the ascension. Few today doubt that this first book is Luke and that Luke and Acts are by the same author.

In Acts 16:10 another personal reference appears. The

author has been describing Paul's second missionary journey. Suddenly, as he tells of Paul's leaving Troas for Macedonia, he writes:

> And when he had seen the vision, immediately *we* sought to go on into Macedonia, concluding that God had called *us* to preach the gospel to them.

From this point on the author says that *we* continued in various missionary activities until Paul left Philippi. The use of the first person plural is resumed when Paul returns to Philippi in his third journey (Acts 20:5), and it continues to the end of the book. The writer seems clearly to be claiming that he was a friend of Paul's, present at some of the events he records, and a preacher himself in the early church.

The tradition that this companion of Paul's was Luke fits in perfectly with the references to Luke in Paul's letters.[2] Luke is never mentioned in the letters of Paul except in connection with places where the author of Acts claims to have been present, and we know of no other friend of Paul's who was present at all the times the word *we* appears.

There is good reason, therefore, to believe that the author of Acts is indeed Luke.[3] If so, we know the following facts about him which have a bearing on the historical accuracy of his report of the first preaching: (1) He was a companion of the great preacher Paul. (2) He was himself a first-century missionary. (Acts 16:10.) (3) He had visited the Jerusalem church, oldest of all Christian churches. (Acts 21:17.) (4) He was acquainted with Philip (Acts 21:8), James (Acts 21:18), and others who had been leaders in the church from the first. And (5) he is writing after what he at least claims was careful investigation. (Luke 1:1-4.)

Two Tests of Luke's Accuracy

How accurate a historian was Luke? Can he be trusted?

At several points Luke's report can be checked against the facts as learned from two other sources: archaeological research, and the letters of Paul.

The archaeological evidence is strongly in Luke's favor. About the turn of the century the British scholar Sir William M. Ramsay set out to retrace Paul's journeys through Asia Minor and Greece. He began this study believing that Acts was a second-century work of little historical value. His discoveries forced a complete change of opinion. For example, contrary to the accepted view at that time, Ramsay became convinced that the city of Iconium was outside the country of Lycaonia as stated in Acts 14:6. Luke is exactly right on this geographic detail.[4] Ramsay found many similar indications of Luke's care and accuracy. Subsequent investigations have tended to confirm Ramsay's discoveries.

Luke's accuracy as a historian may be tested again by comparing his account in Acts with facts from the letters of Paul. It is generally agreed that Luke was not familiar with Paul's letters.[5] He never quoted from them or even mentioned them. Probably Acts was written before Paul's letters had come to be widely regarded as sacred and authoritative. Yet, though Luke is not copying from Paul, Acts and the Epistles agree on a significant number of facts, including details. It is true that at times there do appear to be discrepancies.[6] But the points of agreement are far more numerous and impressive. Here are a few: Both Acts and Galatians mention Barnabas as well known to the churches in Galatia, speak of miracles and of persecutions there, and recall Paul's reception as a god. The Thessalonian letters agree with Acts 17 concerning the presence of a large Gentile element within that church, the hostility of the Jews, the close association of Silas and Timothy with Paul, and the teaching carried on in Thessalonica. The Corinthian letters hint at Paul's reaction to his visit to Athens (1 Corinthians 1:18-25; 2:1-2) described in Acts, and agree with Acts in mentioning his working at a trade in Corinth, in picturing Crispus as a prominent convert, in mentioning Aquila and Priscilla, and in naming Apollos. Other details could be added to the list.

Luke does not write as a twentieth-century "objective" historian. What he is attempting is something far more important for our purposes than would be a systematic, chronological, complete cataloging of facts. As a missionary, Luke gives us rather a series of pictures of the early church, its power and spirit and thought. The accuracy of his report must still be tested, idea by idea, as we see how each concept of the sermons in Acts is related to its Jerusalem setting. But it is of value to us to know that at many points where he can be tested Luke does seem to have been concerned for accurate reporting of the facts.

Luke's Sources of Information

Is it possible to go behind Luke, to penetrate even further back into the "tunnel" between the crucifixion and the New Testament writings? Can one discover and examine the sources which the historian Luke used?

Certainly Luke based his work on written and oral sources. He states this clearly:

> Inasmuch as many have undertaken to compile a narrative of the things which have been accomplished among us, just as they were delivered to us by those who from the beginning were eyewitnesses and ministers of the word, it seemed good to me also, having followed all things closely for

> some time past, to write an orderly account for you, most excellent Theophilus, that you may know the truth concerning the things of which you have been informed. (Luke 1:1-4.)

Luke seems to be claiming, if not that he is himself an eyewitness, at least that he has received information from eyewitnesses. He also professes to be familiar with early Christian documents written even before his Gospel. One of his written sources we possess—the Gospel according to Mark. Again, Luke and Matthew must have known another document, probably a collection of sayings of Jesus, from which each copied passages. This work, which scholars call "Q," now lost, may have been older than any of the four Gospels.

For the second half of Acts, of course, there is no source problem. Luke himself was present at most of the events he describes.

What were his sources of information for the early chapters of Acts, which recount events that occurred perhaps fifty years before the book was written? Several different theories have been proposed. The best supported of these theories groups passages in the first half of Acts around three centers of early Christian tradition as their ultimate source: Jerusalem, Caesarea, and Antioch.

At one point the different views tend to agree. Behind the early chapters, appearing here and there, careful students see hints of a source that goes back to the very cradle of Christianity, to Jerusalem itself.[7]

This is especially striking when we remember three things: Luke himself was very probably a Gentile, not a Jew. Gentile cities like Antioch and Rome soon replaced Jerusalem as centers of Christian activity. And the New Testament was written in Greek and includes ideas which are of Greek origin rather than Hebrew. If, then, these chapters go back to Palestinian thought and language they may be recording pre-written New Testament Christianity, the very earliest ideas of the church.

Luke, who visited the Palestinian cities of Caesarea (Acts 21:8) and Jerusalem (Acts 21:15), seems to have done an amazing thing. W. L. Knox writes:

> Whatever our judgment as to the truth of the narrative of the early chapters of S. Luke's Gospel may be . . . there can be no doubt that S. Luke has succeeded in reproducing in them in a very remarkable degree the atmosphere of the earlier form of Pharisaical piety . . .[8]

It is this atmosphere, this Jewish way of thought as first applied to Jesus, which we are seeking. Stories found only in Luke's Gospel strongly suggests a Jerusalem origin. Some believe that behind the third Gospel lies a written document not only more Palestinian but earlier even than Mark.[9]

This same Jewish stream of thought, perhaps in some primitive Christian manuscript, may lie behind the early chapters of Acts. The Jewish scholar Klausner writes of the first part of Acts:

> . . . there is so much information containing details and names, that it would have been difficult to obtain them by hearsay and to remember them so exactly unless the author had had a written source before him.[10]

The language of these chapters suggests a Hebrew origin. Indeed, one familiar with the Jewish Scriptures who reads these chapters even in English can tell something of this. "He was added to his fathers"; "it came to pass"; "by the hand of" or "mouth of"; "the feet of . . . are at the door"; "his face was going"; "on the face of the earth"; "by the mouth of the sword"; and other such phrases are obviously in the Hebrew manner of speech.

Some language students have gone a step further and have maintained that the early chapters of Acts show traces of having been written originally in Aramaic, the dialect spoken in Palestine in Jesus' day.[11] Others who doubt this have found traces of Aramaic in the language of the sermons of Peter in Acts, the passages with which we are most concerned.[12] Our earliest New Testament books were written, in their present form at least, in Greek. If these early sermons are based on an Aramaic document they do reflect the very beginnings of Christianity.

If such a work in Aramaic did once exist—a record of the earliest days of the church in Jerusalem and Caesarea, dating almost from the time of the events described—and if it could be found, hidden perhaps in some cave near Jerusalem or the Dead Sea, it would be the greatest archaeological discovery of modern times. Bids of millions of dollars from the great libraries of the world would not buy it. Yet it may be that the sermons recorded in the early chapters of Acts echo this very work.

The Sermons Themselves

In general, Acts appears to be the work of an informed historian who wrote on the basis of sources of information coming from the earliest days of the church.

We are concerned primarily with the sermons recorded in the first half of Acts. There are valid reasons for believing that these accurately reflect the thought of the first Christian preaching.

The sermons admittedly are recorded in condensed form. (Acts 2:40.) Their language and style are Luke's.[13] Greek historians are known to have taken greater liberties in their reports of speeches than of events. Yet the Greek historian

Thucydides, who admits to a certain freedom in his accounts of historical addresses, nevertheless states:

> . . . at the same time I endeavored, as nearly as I could, to give the general purport of what was actually said.[14]

Though he may condense and sometimes rephrase Peter's sermons, Luke doubtless endeavors also to give at least "the general purport" of what was said.

At one point Luke's habit in reporting speeches can be tested. We know exactly how he quoted the sayings of Jesus which he found in Mark. It is true that he did sometimes change their setting and recast them in his own style of words. But in general he followed his source closely indeed, almost never altering the meaning of the original saying. If Luke uses the same care in reporting the sermons in Acts, his record is quite trustworthy.

The best evidence that the sermons in Acts are typical of the first Christian preaching is this: comparison of these sermons with other New Testament passages which describe the earliest statements of faith shows a remarkably similar pattern. Here and there throughout the New Testament are strong hints of the content of the primitive gospel, the kind of thing that was preached before a word of the New Testament was written. These passages are much like the sermons in Acts and merit careful study.

There are many references in the Greek New Testament to the *kerygma*, usually translated as the "preaching." We also find the kindred verb "to preach" (*kerusso*). Literally, the words are related to the word for "herald." A herald would proclaim an event that had happened or was about to happen. He might announce the result of a battle or the accession of a king. His task was not that of arguing or persuading but of making a fact known.[15] The first preachers, then, were "heralds of Christ," proclaiming the good news about Him.

The New Testament use of the verb "to preach" is significant. Here are recorded the things men "preached." Most often the preacher is said to have preached "Jesus," or "the Christ," or "the Lord." Sometimes we read of preaching "the kingdom." "Preach the gospel" is a repeated phrase.[16] Men "preach" some account of the deeds of Jesus. And "preaching" often is a call to repentance or forgiveness.

The "preaching," the New Testament use of the word thus suggests, was the announcement of the coming of the Kingdom of God with Jesus as its Lord, confirmed by the cosmic event of His life, death, and resurrection, and related to the salvation which He bestows.

This is exactly the kind of preaching we find described in the first half of Acts.

The British scholar C. H. Dodd, in his book *The Apostolic Preaching and Its Developments,* examines passages in which the Apostle Paul summarizes his "gospel" or his "preaching." [17] Dodd finds that the *kerygma,* the "preaching," as Paul knew it and practiced it, can be summarized in propositions something like these:

> The prophecies are fulfilled, and the new Age is inaugurated by the coming of Christ.
> He was born of the seed of David.
> He died according to the Scriptures, to deliver us out of the present evil age.
> He was buried.
> He rose on the third day according to the Scriptures.
> He is exalted at the right hand of God, as Son of God and Lord of quick and dead.
> He will come again as Judge and Saviour of men.[18]

These propositions would serve almost as well for a summary of the sermons in Acts. The "preaching," as Paul says he first heard it, and these sermons are identical in basic content. If we read between the lines in Paul's Epistles, to discover the gospel behind the New Testament writings, we come to a pattern almost exactly like that of the sermons in Acts.

The witness of passages throughout the New Testament is clear. The sermons in Acts are typical of the kind of thing preached throughout the Christian church from the beginning.

Conclusions

We began this chapter by asking, "How accurate, historically, is the book of Acts in its report of the first Christian preaching?" Do the sermons in the first half of Acts give an accurate picture of what the earliest Christians believed about Christ, even before the New Testament was written?

Investigation has revealed the following facts:

(1) Acts was written by a companion of Paul, a man in a position to know the earliest preaching, himself a first-century missionary.

(2) The author was, at least by first-century standards, a careful and accurate historian.

(3) He made use of primitive Jewish sources which originated in Jerusalem before the era of Gentile Christianity.

(4) The sermons he records are precisely in the pattern of the *kerygma,* the "preaching," which Paul describes in his letters as being the heart of the gospel throughout the early church.

In short, this study has a positive result: Scientific historical research indicates that the sermons in Acts do reflect the thought of the earliest church. They go behind the written books of the New Testament to the very dawn of the Christian faith. They reflect the most exciting period of preaching in all history, the first proclamation of the good news about Jesus. Before the spread of the gospel to the Gentile lands, before the expression of the gospel in Greek language and ideas, before the rise of the myths and legends that produced the apocryphal gospels, this kind of gospel was preached.

"What do you think of the Christ?" This is the primary question. To determine our own answer we have sought the answer closest to the days of Jesus' own earthly life. How did the earliest preachers think of Him? In the sermons in the first half of Acts we find their answers.

CHAPTER 3

JESUS | the Messiah of Jewish Expectation

TO THINK AGAIN the first Christians' thoughts about Jesus one must be prepared to enter a strange world. Mentally the reader must cross five thousand miles, nineteen centuries, and an even wider gulf of ideas. He must leave behind the material world of the scientific twentieth century and enter the exotic world of the Messianic expectation of first-century Jews.

At times it seems a nightmare universe. In it there are

> . . . wonders in the heaven above
> and signs on the earth beneath,
> blood, and fire, and vapor of smoke;
> the sun shall be turned into darkness
> and the moon into blood,
> before the day of the Lord comes,
> the great and manifest day. (Acts 2:19-20.)

Yet this world-view—to us weird and chaotic—was familiar to many downtrodden Jews. Rome might rule now, but the Day of the Lord was at hand. What prophets like Joel had only hinted in the Scripture, contemporary writers described in detail. The author of the now nearly forgotten Jewish book, *The Assumption of Moses,* wrote in words much like those of Acts:

> And the horns of the sun shall be broken and he shall be turned into darkness;
> And the moon shall not give her light, and be turned wholly into blood. (10:5.)[1]

The writers of the Dead Sea scriptures waited for the day when

> The heavens shall thunder loud . . .
> and the gates of [Hell] shall open.*

This is what scholars call the eschatological hope—the expectation of the last times, of the great and terrible Day of the Lord, of the last judgment, and of the final age.

Peter's first sermon recorded in Acts places us squarely in the middle of this world. It is in relation to this expectation of cataclysmic conflict, cosmic judgment, and divine conquest that Peter's opening words set Jesus:

> This is what was spoken by the prophet Joel:
> "And *in the last days* it shall be . . ." (Acts 2:16-17.)

The Expected Cosmic Saviour

Sometimes popular expectation of the last days centered in the figure of a Cosmic Saviour. The writers of the Dead Sea scriptures, for example, looked for the coming of the Prince-Priest "Messiah of Aaron and Israel," [2] who would arise at the end of the present period of tribulation when God had triumphed in the final conflict. Other writings which have survived give more detailed portraits of the one for whom oppressed Jews longed. He would be the Messiah, the Righteous and Elect One. He was now concealed in heaven beside the throne of God. Soon he would be revealed as the Conquerer of Satan and his hosts, the Judge of angels and men, the Saviour of the penitent elect.

In caves near the Dead Sea archaeologists have recently discovered eight Aramaic copies of an "apocalyptic" work

* "The Book of Hymns," Psalm V. From: *The Dead Sea Scriptures* by Theodor H. Gaster, copyright © 1956 by Theodor H. Gaster, reprinted by permission of Doubleday & Company, Inc.

called "The Book of Enoch," [3] previously known in Ethiopic and Greek versions. Though much of it seems weird to modern readers its ideas were probably quite familiar and meaningful to Peter's hearers. In words like these it pictures the kind of Messiah of which downtrodden Jews dreamed:

> This is the Son of Man who hath righteousness, with whom dwelleth righteousness, and who reveals all the treasures of that which is hidden, because the Lord of Spirits hath chosen him . . . And he will put down the kings from their thrones and kingdoms because they do not extol and praise him, nor thankfully acknowledge whence the kingdom was bestowed upon them. (Enoch 46:3-5.)

This conquering Messiah was said to have existed before all creation.

> . . . and he will be the light of the Gentiles and the hope of those who are troubled of heart . . . And for this reason has he been chosen and hidden before Him before the creation of the world and for evermore. And the wisdom of the Lord of Spirits hath revealed him to the holy and righteous . . . (Enoch 48:4-7.)

From his heavenly throne he will judge kings and even angels.

> Ye mighty kings who will dwell on the earth, ye shall have to behold Mine Elect, how he sits on the throne of glory and judges Azazel, and all his associates, and all his hosts in the name of the Lord of Spirits. (Enoch 55:4.)

This picture of the Cosmic Judge of Angels and men may be foreign to our minds. But refined and reborn it played its part in the earliest portraits drawn by the first preachers as they proclaimed the heavenly Messiah, Jesus. The titles and attributes to be discussed below indicate some of the parallels between the Jewish expectation of the Cosmic Deliverer and Peter's description of Jesus.

The Title "Messiah" or "Christ"

Certain titles used by Peter make clear the identification of Jesus with the awaited Divine Judge. Of these, by far the most important is the one translated *Messiah,* the *Christ,* the *Anointed One.* (Enoch 48:10; 52:4; compare Acts 2:36; 3:20.)

Jesus is so frequently called "Christ" today that the great meaning of the title is often forgotten. Indeed, for many Christians "Christ" has become little more than a name, like "Jesus." Jesus was the name the Child of Mary was given at birth. It was a common name, actually the same as "Joshua" in another form. There were many men in Palestine named Jesus; but Peter's proclamation of Jesus as the "Christ" was a startling announcement. This is the climax of the first recorded Christian sermon. Everything else builds up to it.

> Let all the house of Israel therefore know assuredly that God has made him both Lord and *Christ,* this Jesus whom you crucified. (Acts 2:36.)

Indeed, so early and so widespread was the identification of Jesus as the "Christ" that New Testament writers tend to take it for granted. Luke himself often uses "Jesus" and "Christ" interchangeably or couples them together as "Jesus Christ." The first sermons, however, focus attention on this title "Christ." Peter's great announcement about Jesus is that "God has made him . . . Christ."

What does this title mean?

"Christ," of course, is the Greek form of the Hebrew word "Messiah," which means "the Anointed One." Old Testament anointing and its relationship to Jesus will be discussed in the next chapter. However, though the word "anoint" occurs frequently, nowhere in the Old Testament is it used to describe a promised Saviour of the world. By other names such a Saviour is promised, but never is He called "Messiah" or "Christ." [4]

The title, therefore, must be understood not in the light of the Old Testament Scriptures alone but in the light of Jewish "apocalyptic" writings of the time. In them many of Peter's hearers had heard of a "Christ" such as he described. The Dead Sea scriptures show that their authors dreamed of a coming "Messiah"—perhaps two "Messiahs"—a heavenly Prince and Priest. The oldest such use of this title yet found is in the Book of Enoch, from which we have been quoting.[5] The awaited "Elect One," "the Son of Man," is called in Enoch "the Messiah," "the Christ." Whatever else the title meant, when Peter called Jesus "the Christ" he was identifying Him with such a figure as Enoch's Cosmic Judge, the One who would "bring light to the Gentiles," before whom angels and men would bow the knee, the One whose appearing would usher in the glorious age of the final triumph of God.

This "Christ" whom Enoch describes is no ordinary mortal, however much he may be called a "Son of Man." He is modeled on that "son of man" mentioned in Daniel:

> I saw in the night visions,
>
> and behold, with the clouds of heaven
>   there came one like *a son of man,*
> and he came to the Ancient of Days
>   and was presented before him.
> And to him was given dominion
>   and glory and kingdom,
> that all peoples, nations, and languages
>   should serve him;
> his dominion is an everlasting dominion,
>   which shall not pass away,

and his kingdom one
that shall not be destroyed.
(Daniel 7:13-14.)

Enoch goes beyond Daniel, however, in describing this "son of man" who is called "the Christ." His "Christ" was in the presence of God before creation began. (Enoch 48:3.) He is conqueror over kings and mighty ones. (Enoch 46:4-5.) He is "the Elect One" who judges and destroys all sin. (Enoch 45:5.) This is what Peter meant when he called Jesus "the Christ."

An especially important parallel is that in both Enoch and Acts "the Christ" is called *the Righteous One,* the living embodiment of the righteous character of God. (Acts 3:14; Enoch 38:2.)

The Title "the Righteous One"

The Dead Sea scriptures, recently discovered in the Judean desert, give new witness to the importance of the idea of "righteousness" in the Jewish Messianic hope. The strange Jewish community which wrote and studied these books seems to have thought of itself as God's army, preparing itself for the final battle between God and Satan. In one of their books, called *The War of the Sons of Light with the Sons of Darkness,* it is promised that in the end God will send Michael, "the mighty, ministering angel," to bring the final victory.

> The rule of Michael will be exalted among the angels . . .
> Righteousness shall flourish in heaven.*

* From *The Dead Sea Scriptures* by Theodor H. Gaster (p. 304), copyright © 1956 by Theodor H. Gaster, reprinted by permission of Doubleday & Company, Inc.

The community revered this memory and perhaps awaited the return of "the Teacher of Righteousness."

Enoch uses the very words, "the Righteous One," as a title for the Cosmic Deliverer.

> And when the *Righteous One* shall appear before the eyes of the elect righteous . . . Where then will be the dwelling of sinners . . . ? (Enoch 38:2.)
>
> And after this *the Righteous* and Elect *One* will cause the house of his congregation to appear . . .
> And these mountains will not stand fast as the earth before his righteousness . . . (Enoch 53:6-7.)

The title, "the Righteous One," is used of Jesus nowhere in the New Testament except in the sermons in Acts. (Acts 3:14; 7:52.) Later it was abandoned for what seemed richer titles for Jesus. The sermons bear witness to its place in the days of the Jewish beginnings of the church.[6]

Strange as it may seem, when the first preachers called Jesus "the Righteous One" they were by no means simply calling Him an extraordinarily good man. They were identifying Him as the longed-for Cosmic Being, who quite possibly existed from before creation "at the right hand of God" in heaven, the predestined Judge and Conqueror, miraculously endowed with the righteous character of God.

Hidden Existence With God

That the first preachers thought of Jesus as the Heavenly Deliverer is made clear by titles such as "the Christ" and "the Righteous One." It is also shown by their picture of Jesus as now enjoying an existence with God in heaven, hidden from human view.

Peter pictures Jesus at the right hand of God (Acts 2:34),

in the special position of heavenly favor. He has been received in heaven until the time for the restoration of the divine order. (Acts 3:21.)

This idea of a concealed Messiah is not the usual promise of the Old Testament itself. However, Peter's hearers would be familiar with it. Of "the Son of Man" the book of Enoch says:

> And for this reason has he been chosen and hidden before Him before the creation of the world and for evermore. (Enoch 48:6; compare Enoch 62:7.)

Other books have the same strange picture. A later book called 4 Ezra pictures the Jewish Messiah as rising at last from the sea, and adds:

> . . . this is he whom the Most High is keeping many ages [(and through whom he will deliver his creation . . .)] (4 Ezra 13:26.)

Other references to a concealed Messiah might be noted.[7]

If Peter did indeed mean to connect Jesus with this popular Jewish idea of a Saviour now concealed but to be revealed to His people miraculously, one startling conclusion seems possible: From the beginning Jesus may have been thought of not simply as the human son of Joseph and Mary but as pre-existent, "hidden from the beginning" with God like Enoch's Elect One. Much later John was to write, "In the beginning was the Word, and the Word was with God." (John 1:1.) Something of this idea was latent from the first.

The Age of Restoration

Another idea which connects the sermons of Peter with the popular Jewish hope of the last days is that of the "restoration of all things."[8] This age of restoration or "times of refreshing" (Acts 3:19) will be ushered in by the revelation of the now concealed Messiah.

The need for this restoration had long been felt. Through Adam's sin even the ground had been cursed. (Genesis 3:17.) Prophet after prophet had dreamed of a redeemed nature at the end of time. Eden would be restored; the desert would rejoice and blossom as the rose. (Isaiah 35:1, K.J.V.) Some pictured this restitution of the original state as coming at the beginning of Messiah's reign (Enoch 45:5), others at the end (4 Ezra 7:30-31).

Against this background we can understand Peter's reference to "restoration" and "times of refreshing." Jesus, the Cosmic Deliverer, is to be the Great Restorer of that which Adam's sin destroyed.

The Judge

One of the clearest connections between the Christ of the early chapters of Acts and the Cosmic Deliverer of popular expectation appears when Peter explicitly calls Jesus the chosen *Judge*.

Preaching to Cornelius and his household Peter declares:

> And he commanded us to preach to the people, and to testify that he is the one ordained by God to be judge of the living and the dead. (Acts 10:42.)

The apostle pictures Jesus as a supernatural Judge presiding over the final judgment day, judging not only those now on earth, but also those now dead who will appear before the heavenly tribunal. This idea of the final judgment lies behind the exhortation to repent and to receive salvation, which forms a repeated part of the sermons attributed to Peter. (Acts 2:38; 3:19; 5:31.)

The idea of universal judgment was the heart of the popular expectation among Jews of the first century. It was a standard part of the strange, unearthly realm of "apocalyptic" thought. A Jewish book called 2 Baruch prophesies:

> My Messiah will convict him [the evil leader or Satan] of all his impieties, and will gather and set before him all the works of his hosts. And afterwards he will put him to death, and protect the rest of My people. (2 Baruch 40: 1-2; compare 72:3.)

Other books of the time abound in descriptions of the final judgment. Angels, devils, Israel, the Gentiles, the living, and the dead are all judged by the Messiah. Peter identifies Jesus as this expected Messiah-Judge.

The Old Testament also abounds in pictures of a final judgment. (Isaiah 2:4; Psalm 9:5,7-8; Joel 3:12; Malachi 3:5; 4:1-3, etc.) But in the Old Testament it is God Himself who is the Judge.[9] This was no light title, then, to be bestowed upon the man Jesus. It was a long step toward the full recognition of His divinity.

The Saviour

Against the background of this picture of Jesus as the supernatural Christ, now at the right hand of God and soon to be revealed as the Righteous Judge of angels and men, we may understand another of the first ideas about Jesus: He is the *Saviour* of the penitent elect.

The proclamation of the Messiah was the proclamation of salvation. In every sermon of Peter's this forms part of the climax. The title Saviour is used but once (Acts 5:31), but the idea is everywhere in the kerygma, the preaching. It is the heart of the message.

Whom does the Messiah save? Two answers are repeatedly given: the elect people, and those spiritually fit. The Gentile Luke does not fail to record that the first Jewish preachers proclaimed salvation to the elect race, Israel.

> God exalted him at his right hand . . . to give repentance to Israel . . . (Acts 5:31; compare 2:39; 3:25.)

But though salvation is associated with the chosen people, repentance and faith are necessary for its reception. "Repent!" is the cry of every sermon. (Acts 2:38; 3:19; 5:31.) This repentance is bestowed by Jesus Himself. (Acts 3:26; 5:31.) Therefore salvation is for those only who stand in a special relationship to Him, the Saviour-Judge.

> For there is no other name under heaven given among men by which we must be saved. (Acts 4:12; compare 3:16; 10:43.)

The accuracy of Luke is again made plain, for this concept is quite in agreement with the Jewish hope. Rabbis taught that

> If Israel would together repent for a whole day, the redemption by Messiah would ensue. (Targum of Micah 6:8.)

Enoch had pictured the promised Saviour in these terms:

> For in those days the Elect One shall arise
> And he shall choose the righteous and holy from among them:
> For the day has drawn nigh that they should be saved.
> (Enoch 51:1-2; compare 45:3-6; Testament of Levi 2; Psalms of Solomon 17:33, etc.)

Judgment and salvation are both parts of the same picture. The Judge is also the Saviour, for He who condemns Satan and all the enemies of the righteous will destroy these enemies and thus deliver the penitent elect.

That God Himself was frequently pictured in Jewish writings as the *Saviour* [10] is another indication of the path by which the church was to come to know who Jesus really is.

Jesus and the Spirit

Finally, in connection with the idea of Jesus as the Deliverer of Jewish expectation must be noted the relationship proclaimed by the first preachers as existing between Jesus and the *Spirit* of God. Like the Messiah of the common Jewish hope, He was said to be anointed with that Spirit (Acts 10:38) and to be the One who now pours out that Spirit upon His people (Acts 2:33).

The pouring out of the Spirit as a sure sign that "the last days" had come introduces the first Christian sermon:

> . . . but this is what was spoken by the prophet Joel:
>
> "And in the last days it shall be, God declares,
> that I will pour out my Spirit upon all flesh . . ."
> (Acts 2:16-17.)

Joel was not the only writer who had foreseen this event. "Enoch" sings of the Elect One:

> And the spirit of righteousness was poured out upon him. (Enoch 62:2.)

The Dead Sea scriptures foretold of man that in the Messianic age, God

> will sprinkle upon him a spirit of truth, like water for impurity.[11]

And in language almost as beautiful as that of the Old Testament itself, the Testament of Judah prophesies:

And after these things shall a star arise to you from Jacob
in peace [compare Acts 10:36 and Numbers 24:17],
And a man shall arise [from my seed], like the sun of
righteousness,
Walking with the sons of men in meekness and righteousness;
And no sin shall be found in him.
And the heavens shall be opened unto him,
To pour out the spirit, (even) the blessing of the Holy
Father;
And He shall pour out the spirit of grace upon you;
And ye shall be unto Him sons in truth,
And ye shall walk in His commandments first and last.

Then shall the sceptre of my kingdom shine forth;
And from your root shall arise a stem;
And from it shall grow a rod of righteousness to the
Gentiles,
To judge and to save all that call upon the Lord.
(The Testament of the Twelve Patriarchs, The Testament of Judah 24:1-6.)

Surely this is what Peter meant when he preached Jesus!

It is precisely this dual relationship to the Spirit of God which sets the Anointed One apart from all the rest of the universe: He is anointed with the Spirit; and He bestows the Spirit. For Peter the fact of Jesus' power, His proclamation of peace, His judgeship, and His righteousness all flow from the Spirit, which is the Spirit of power, peace, wisdom, and righteousness. It is through this Spirit that He is the Saviour of men. And this Spirit is wholly divine; it is the Spirit of the transcendent God.

Conclusions

What does this first-century Jewish picture of Jesus mean to us in the twentieth century?

At first it seems utterly foreign. In a day of exotic speculations Jesus was described in terms derived, in part at least, from the desperate hope of the oppressed little Jewish nation. Words and ideas in the first sermons—*Righteous One, Judge, Saviour, Spirit*—repeatedly connect Jesus with "the last days." Jesus was pictured in terms like those used of the expected angelic "Messiah," now hidden with God in heaven, who was supposed to deliver Israel by grinding their oppressors to powder, judging even angels and devils in righteousness, and ushering in the final glorious age.

Yet primitive and incomplete as this picture of Jesus is, it has meaning for today:

(1) It shows the historical accuracy of Luke's report. Luke himself was a Gentile Christian writing perhaps fifty years after Pentecost. In his Gospel he tends to emphasize such ideas about Jesus as that He was the Great Physician, the Friend of Women, and the Light to the Gentiles, rather than picturing Him as the Cosmic Judge. But in Acts he has reported Peter's sermons in language and thought that reflect the hopes of troubled Jerusalem. Over and over the picture of Jesus given in these sermons can be paralleled in the Jewish "apocalyptic" writings. Acts really does record the first ideas about Jesus.

(2) The idea of Jesus as the Heavenly Deliverer of otherwise hopeless peoples is not everywhere irrelevant today. A refugee from a country now dominated by Russia once said to the writer, "We have no hope. Frankly, at first we hoped for war. We hoped America would deliver us with her bombs. But when Russia got the Bomb, too, then we knew war would simply mean annihilation. Now we have nothing, no hope at all." Perhaps it is no wonder that thousands in Europe are examining again this "eschatological" picture of Christ who is more powerful than all tyrants. Nor can the

American Christian afford to forget that his own hope of salvation lies not in his bombs or his gadgets but in the power of this transcendent Christ.

(3) The idea of Jesus as the Cosmic Judge stands ready to demolish any weak modern perversion of Christianity. "Gentle Jesus, meek and mild" may be a useful picture for children. But the Christ of the earliest Christians is a conquering Heavenly Messiah who cannot be trifled with. He judges and He is to be obeyed. It is precisely because He is not only human but has the supernatural power of the Spirit that He can save. Jesus is transcendent, terrible toward sin, worthy of the uncompromising trust and loyalty He demands, a Being who is divine in a quite special way.

Postscript

This is not the whole story. The Jesus of the earliest Christians is not simply the Jewish apocalyptic "Christ." The earliest preachers took what was best in such works as Enoch, but much they transformed and much they left behind.

For one thing, such Jewish books seem always to have come from periods of despair as a kind of last hope. There is nothing of this despair in Peter's preaching. The longed-for age of the Messiah has already dawned! The work of Christ is shouted in triumph as present fact: "This *is* what was spoken by the prophet . . ."

There are other differences between the Christ of Peter's sermons and the Messiah of Jewish hope. The Deliverer of Jewish expectation appears as a bloody avenger of Judea's wrongs. Nothing of this vindictiveness is in Acts. The weird speculations about demons and demigods found in many Jewish writings are abandoned. "The Elect One" of Enoch is neither man nor God but some undefined super-angel.

Nothing of this fantasy appears in Acts. The memory of the human Jesus was too fresh on the one hand, and the consciousness of His transcendence was too high on the other.

No, for a more complete picture of the Christ of the earliest Christians we must look deeper. Behind the queer Jewish books popular in the first century were other books far richer in meaning, far loftier in hope. For more adequate words to describe Jesus the earliest Christians turned to the Jewish Scriptures themselves.

CHAPTER 4

JESUS | the Fulfiller of the Old Testament

IT WAS THE AMAZING CLAIM of the infant Christian church that the whole of the Jewish Scripture was written for them. If one really wants to know what the first Christians thought about Jesus the key lies partly in these words of Peter, ". . . this is what was spoken by the prophet . . ." (Acts 2:16.) Jesus was for the earliest Christians the Fulfillment and Fulfiller of all the Old Testament hope.

This is not to deny the truth of what has been said in the preceding chapter. Jesus was indeed thought of in terms derived from such strange books as Enoch and some of the Dead Sea scriptures. He was indeed pictured as the Cosmic Saviour whose coming had ushered in the final age, who was now concealed in heaven, and who would judge the world in terrible righteousness. But even the books which developed these ideas, sometimes in such curious fashion, were at their best also based on the Old Testament Scripture. And it is the consistent testimony of the New Testament that the early church, from the very first days after the Resurrection, went behind the speculations of Jewish thinkers of their own day to a new and glorious understanding of the Old Testament.

The Importance of the Old Testament

The first Christians turned to the Old Testament for many different ideas to describe Jesus.

They thought of Jesus as the promised King described by the psalmist in these words:

> The Lord says to my lord:
> "Sit at my right hand,
> till I make your enemies
> your footstool."
>
> The Lord sends forth from Zion
> your mighty scepter.
> Rule in the midst of your foes!
> (Psalm 110:1-2; compare Acts 2:34-35.)

They called Jesus the Promised Prophet, the Second Moses:

> I will raise up for them a prophet like you [Moses] from among their brethren; and I will put my words in his mouth. (Deuteronomy 18:18; compare Acts 3:22.)

They found in Him the fulfillment of the mission of Israel:

> The stone which the builders rejected has become the chief cornerstone. (Psalm 118:22; compare Acts 4:11.)

> Behold my servant . . . he was wounded for our transgressions. (Isaiah 42:1; 53:5; compare Acts 3:13.)

It was in passages such as these that the first preachers found words to proclaim the meaning of Jesus. In fact, it was not only to a few isolated passages that they turned but to the entire Book. Nor was it simply to descriptions of the Old Testament's Messiah that they turned but to phrases used of God Himself.

Over and over the sermons of Peter declare that Jesus is the One to whom the Old Testament prophecies pointed:

> To him all the prophets bear witness. (Acts 10:43; compare Acts 2:16; 3:18; 3:21-22; 3:24.)

They not only stated that Jesus was the fulfillment of the Old Testament prophecies but they supported this claim with numerous quotations from the Scripture. The sermons of Peter in Acts include sixty verses. There are sixteen quotations from the Old Testament in twenty-four verses of these sixty. The sermons are a mosaic of Old Testament references, used by Peter to describe Christ. One simply cannot fully understand this or any other part of the New Testament apart from the Old. The actual event of Jesus' life told them *who* He was. But it was the Old Testament which told them *what* He was—and *why*.

In giving this picture of these early Christian sermons, Acts seems to be quite accurate. Many of the Scripture passages quoted in Peter's sermons are found again and again scattered through the rest of the New Testament. All the writers echo this witness that Jesus is the Promised One. Indeed, several scholars have argued that the first book of the Christian church, written before any of the New Testament, was a collection of Old Testament quotations applied to Christ.[1]

Methods of Interpreting the Old Testament

We need to remember that what the words of Scripture meant to first-century Jewish Christians may have been something quite different from what these words mean to us. Three methods of interpretation should be recognized:

First, modern interpreters of an Old Testament passage ask, quite properly, "What did these words mean originally to the inspired writer and to those who heard him in his own day?"

Second, Jewish rabbis of the days of the early church gave very different meanings to these same words, often interpreting them fancifully and allegorically.

Third—and this is most important for our purpose—the

primitive Christians found new meanings, broader and far richer than those of which either the first hearers or the Jewish rabbis ever dreamed. They completely reinterpreted the entire Old Testament, saw every word of it as pointing to Jesus and every fact about Him foreshadowed in it. It was not so much that this or that detail seemed to apply to Christ. He was the Fulfillment of the whole book, and thus any of its statements might testify to Him.

Paul contrasts this Christian interpretation of Scripture with that of the Jews of his day, saying that the eyes of the Jews' minds seemed veiled as they read the Old Testament:

> . . . for to this day, when they read the old covenant, that same veil remains unlifted, because only through Christ is it taken away. Yes, to this day whenever Moses is read a veil lies over their minds; but when a man turns to the Lord the veil is removed. (2 Corinthians 3:14-16.)
>
> For all the promises of God find their Yes in Him. (2 Corinthians 1:20.)

For the first Christians all Scripture pointed to Christ.

Where did this new understanding of the Scripture originate? It is the witness of Luke that it came in the earliest ecstatic days of the church, from the Risen Christ. (Luke 24:27.)

As we examine the Old Testament quotations and ideas applied to Jesus in the sermons of Peter we shall seek to understand them as they were understood by the earliest Christians in the days following the Resurrection.

The Kingly Title "Christ"

A focal point of the earliest preaching was the proclamation that Jesus was the promised Messiah-King, great David's greater Son.

Around this central concept various ideas and titles cluster. Among these are the title "Christ" (Acts 2:36), the concept of Jesus as the promised "descendant" of David (Acts 2:29-30), and the title "Lord" (Acts 2:36).

What did these three ideas mean to the earliest church?

"Christ" was the glorious title applied to Jesus first by Peter and then by all the church. (Mark 8:29.) We have seen the way in which this title as used in contemporary Jewish literature suggested the Cosmic Judge of all the earth.

In its Hebrew Old Testament origins, however, the word is derived from the verb "to anoint." "Christ" is the Greek translation of "Messiah," meaning literally "the Anointed One."

Anointing was the ceremony by which a man was set apart as king. Samuel anointed Saul king. (1 Samuel 10:1.) David was anointed king. (1 Samuel 16:13; 2 Samuel 2:4.) Solomon was anointed king. (1 Kings 1:39.) Whatever else the title "the Anointed One" meant as used of Jesus, surely it meant that He was *the King*. Not Herod on his "Quisling" throne (nor even Caesar, Emperor of Rome), but Jesus of Nazareth was the King. All that Saul and David and Solomon were meant to be and never quite became, all the kingdom of God that never quite appeared in the Hebrew kingdom, has now been realized in Jesus.

The title "the Anointed One" had more than political significance. Anointing set aside a man for a special task, consecrated him to a divine calling. The "Servant of the Lord" was anointed to preach. (Isaiah 61:1.) Priests and the holy instruments of worship were set apart by anointing. (Exodus 30:30; 40:10-15.) "The Anointed One" was the King who stood in special relationship to God—holy, consecrated to a divine task, anointed "with the Holy Spirit and with power" to rule and to save the world. (Acts 10:38.)

The Kingly Title "Son of David"

The concept of Jesus as the descendant of David (Acts 2:30) is also to be understood in the light of Old Testament prophecy of an Ideal King. What this meant to Jewish hearers was not simply that Jesus was physically descended from David. Doubtless He was so descended, but so were others. It meant that He was seen as the Fulfillment of the kind of promise God made through Nathan about David's son:

> I will raise up your son after you . . . and I will establish the throne of his kingdom for ever. I will be his father, and he shall be my son. (2 Samuel 7:12-14.)

Solomon was disappointing. He proved not to be the King who should rule eternally as the Son of God. In Jesus the inspired community saw David's greater Son—all that Solomon failed to be.

It was not some courthouse record which gave rise to the concept of Jesus as the Son of David. There was no single established tradition concerning Jesus' ancestry. The genealogical tables in Matthew 1 and Luke 3 are quite different, probably because they were drawn up much later in independent efforts to document what had long been preached. Jesus was called "the Son of David" not simply because men knew of His physical descent but because He was the Fulfillment of the ancient promises. When the first preachers called Jesus "the Son of David" they meant that He was the One of whom generations had sung:

> The Lord swore to David a sure oath
> from which he will not turn back:
> "One of the sons of your body
> I will set on your throne."
> (Psalm 132:11.)

The Kingly Title "Lord"

Perhaps the most interesting of the Messianic titles given to Jesus by the Jerusalem church is the title *Lord*. Those today who use it thoughtlessly Sunday after Sunday hardly realize the original significance of this word.

What was the earliest creed of the Christian church? Is it possible to go even further back than the Apostles' Creed to the very first formula of the Christian faith? The continental scholar Oscar Cullmann thinks we can.[2] He examines the oldest documents and the earliest books of the church and traces back the first confessions used in baptism, worship, and persecution. And always he arrives at one original formula: "Jesus Christ is Lord." This was the first Christian creed.

This announcement is the climax of the first sermon recorded in Acts. It is the final proclamation of Peter's sermon on the Day of Pentecost:

> Let all the house of Israel therefore know assuredly that God has made him both Lord and Christ, this Jesus whom you crucified. (Acts 2:36; compare Acts 7:59; 10:36.)

If the title was seldom used in Jesus' earthly life,[3] there is good reason to believe that it was used soon after.[4] Paul seems to have known the word as part of the original Christian confession. He assumes that his readers will understand when he says that to "confess with your lips that Jesus is Lord" leads to salvation. (Romans 10:9.) Surely reference to this creed is the meaning of the otherwise strange statement ". . . no one can say 'Jesus is Lord' except by the Holy Spirit." (1 Corinthians 12:3.) A twentieth-century Christian may use the title thoughtlessly, but no first-century Christian could. Many scholars think that Philippians 2:5-11, with the climax ". . . and every tongue confess that Jesus Christ is Lord . . . ," is part of one of the first Christian hymns.[5]

The clearest indication that the title "Lord" as applied to Jesus comes from the earliest Christians lies in Paul's cry *Marantha,* which means "Our Lord, come!" (1 Corinthians 16:22.) Though writing in Greek to Greek-speaking Christians, Paul repeats this phrase in Aramaic. Back to the language of the Jerusalem church he goes for this prayer, knowing that even his Greek readers will be familiar with it in that original form, "Our Lord, come!" This, from the beginning, was the petition of the church.

What did Jewish Christians mean when they called Jesus "Lord"?

First, they meant that Jesus was the One seated at the right hand of God, of whom the psalmist sang:

> The Lord says to my lord:
> "Sit at my right hand,
> till I make your enemies
> your footstool."
> . . . .
> The Lord has sworn
> and will not change his mind,
> "You are a priest for ever
> after the order of Melchizedek."
> (Psalm 110:1,4.)

No other passage of the Old Testament is so often quoted in the New! Its picture of the King who is co-regent with God, exalted to the place of highest honor with God, and who is also an eternal Priest, seemed to the first Christians the Old Testament's finest portrait of Jesus. Twenty-four times the Psalm is quoted or alluded to. It is found in the first three Gospels, Acts, four of the Epistles of Paul, Hebrews, First Peter, and Revelation. There are also many other references to Jesus as at "the right hand of God." Jesus was the King who shared God's throne. So often did the Jewish Christians quote this Psalm that the rabbis who debated with them refused for 250 years to admit that it had any connection with the expected Messiah. For first-century Christians, Psalm 110 was the favorite picture of Jesus, the Heavenly King and Priest, to whose service they offered themselves gladly (verse 3)—servants of the *Lord*.

There was an infinitely larger connotation to the word. "The Lord" was an Old Testament name for God Himself![6] Was Peter on the Day of Pentecost already calling Jesus God? At least it must be said that *Lord* was a sacred word, one which pious Jews would not even bestow on the Emperor himself. The title was a step in the direction of the full realization of the deity of Jesus. That they would use it of a man recently crucified as a criminal seems incredible, but it is true. Jesus alone could be called *Lord*.

The three titles discussed thus far in this chapter ("Christ," "Son of David," and "Lord") all cluster about the concept of Jesus as the Fulfillment of the hope of centuries for Israel's True King. But they point to something more than an earthly ruler, however ideal. In many a "Messianic" prophecy in the Old Testament it is God Himself who is to come and to rule. The expected kingdom is heavenly and supernatural. The kingdom age is the era not simply of peace and prosperity but of the righteous reign of God in triumph. All this, said the first preachers, has come true in the person and work of Jesus.

The Promised Prophet

Jesus was—and is still—called the King. Another idea about Jesus suggested in the preaching of Peter is so transcended by later understanding of Him that it is now nearly forgotten. It is the picture of Jesus as a Second Joshua, the Successor of Moses, the Promised *Prophet,* leading His people into the new age.

This idea is made clearest in the second sermon of Peter:

> Moses said, "The Lord God will raise up for you a prophet from your brethren as he raised me up. You shall listen to him in whatever he tells you. And it shall be that every soul that does not listen to that prophet shall be destroyed . . ." (Acts 3:22-23.)

This quotation is based on Deuteronomy 18:15-19. Originally these words may have referred to the whole succession of God's prophets. But our concern is to understand what they meant to the Jerusalem church.

In the days between the Old Testament and the New it seemed that the age of prophets had ended. Only the hope remained that the words of Malachi—whose prophecy ends our Old Testament—would some day be fulfilled:

> Behold, I will send you Elijah the prophet before the great and terrible day of the Lord comes. (Malachi 4:5.)

Even John the Baptist would not accept the title of prophet, for there were to be no more prophets till that One should come who would usher in the Messianic Age. (John 1:20-21.)

The Promised One would be the Last Great Prophet.[7] The Dead Sea Scrolls have recently given new witness to this Jewish hope,[8] one fragment quoting as Messianic prophecy the very passage from Deuteronomy which Peter quotes about the Promised Prophet. The Jewish historian Josephus, a contemporary of Luke, tells of efforts by false messiahs to fulfill this prophecy literally. In Acts 5:36 we have mention of a false messiah named Theudas whose rebellion in New Testament days failed. Apparently it is of this same false claimant to be the Messiah that Josephus writes:

> Theudas persuaded a great part of the people to take their effects with them, and follow him to the river Jordan; for he told them he was a prophet, and that he would, by his own command, divide the river, and afford them an easy passage over it. (Antiquities XX, v, 1.)

That is to say, this false Messiah claimed to be the successor of Moses, another Joshua, duplicating the feat of Joshua in parting the Jordan River. (Joshua 3.) Josephus tells of another false Messiah called "the prophet from Egypt" who claimed to make walls fall as Joshua did. He

> advised the multitude of the common people to go along with him to the Mount of Olives . . . he would show them from hence how, at his command, the walls of Jerusalem would fall down. (Antiquities XX, viii, 6.)

Thus he, too, would show himself the successor of Moses, the second Joshua, the Promised Prophet of the Last Age.

To Jewish hearers, then, to call Jesus "the prophet like unto Moses" was to make a startling claim. It was not simply to say that Jesus was one more in the noble succession of Isaiah and Jeremiah and Malachi. It was to claim in some sense that Jesus was the Messiah Himself.

As the Second Moses, the New Joshua, Jesus is called the Author of life (Acts 3:15), the Leader or Prince (Acts 5:31) —translations of the Greek word *archegos,* also translated in Hebrews 12:2 as the Pioneer. The Word in secular Greek is used of heroes who with great deeds founded nations and gave them laws.

What these first preachers were saying about Jesus, then, was this: That as Moses and Joshua had led heroically in the establishment of the redeemed community Israel, had given them their laws, made them a nation, and led them into the promised land, so in a far larger sense Jesus was the beloved Prince and Pioneer of the new Israel—their Hero in the battle with Satan, their new Lawgiver, the Revealer of God's will—who had led them not across the Jordan but across the river of death, into the promised age of life.

This Jewish concept of the meaning of Jesus, valuable as it was, was soon to be replaced by ideas with more meaning to the Gentile world. It reappears in only one other book of the New Testament, the Epistle to the Hebrews. (2:10; 12:2.)

The Rejected Stone

Peter saw Jesus as the One in whom the historic mission of Israel was at last being fulfilled. This interpretation lies behind his quotation of Psalm 118:22. Preaching Christ crucified and risen, Peter tells his judges: "This is the stone which was rejected by you builders, but which has become the head of the corner." (Acts 4:11; compare Psalm 118:22.)

The application of this passage to the Messiah was a strange idea. Jewish rabbis of Peter's day all interpreted the Psalm to mean the nation Israel, so often despised and conquered by its neighbors but in the divine plan destined to be the most important nation for the Kingdom of God. In this understanding the rabbis were in a sense quite right. This was what the psalmist meant. But we must think our way back into the Jerusalem church in the first ecstatic days of the Resurrection experiences to feel the astounding boldness of their new proclamation. It mattered little that these words had never before been associated with the Davidic Messiah. What Israel had never succeeded in becoming, Jesus was! The mission of Israel was fulfilled in Him.

So firmly was this relationship between Jesus and the passage in Psalm 118 established and so early was it preached that the Psalm is applied to Him all through the New Testament in otherwise varying books. (Mark 12:10; Acts 4:11; Ephesians 2:20; 1 Peter 2:6-8; compare Romans 9:33.)

The Holy and Righteous One

A strain of Old Testament thought which if not explicitly connected with Jesus in the sermons of Peter in Acts is at least implied in interpreting Him, is that drawn from Hebrew cultic worship. Jesus is called *the Holy One.* (Acts 3:14; compare Mark 1:24; John 6:69.) A glance at a concordance is all that is necessary to see that this takes the reader into the thought forms of Exodus, Leviticus, and Ezekiel. "Holiness" is the Old Testament word for cultic purity, separation from the world. Again there is the title *the Righteous One* or *the Just One* (Acts 3:14), implying piety, fulfillment of God's will. Perhaps in this word and in the concept of Jesus as the Greater Moses there may be hints of a relationship being established between Jesus and the law. Years later Paul was to work out the doctrine of salvation through faith in Christ rather than through the works of the Mosaic law, but the seeds of this doctrine were planted earlier. Priests were anointed as well as kings, and the use of Psalm 110 was soon to provide Scriptural background for the thought that Jesus is "a Priest forever," again connecting Him with Jewish worship. The repeated references to forgiveness are specifically related to the Old Testament Scripture and thus presumably to the sacrificial system:[9]

> To him all the prophets bear witness that every one who believes in him receives forgiveness of sins through his name. (Acts 10:43.)

What priest and sacrifice sought to do, Jesus did.

Jesus and the God of the Old Testament

The final Old Testament idea implicitly if not explicitly related to Jesus is the most amazing of all. Jesus is described in terms which the Old Testament uses of the Messiah, the Prophet, and the People of God. But over and over titles and functions are ascribed to Jesus which are not so much those of the Old Testament Messiah as of the Old Testament *God.* Did Peter on the Day of Pentecost announce that Jesus was God? No, the doctrine of the Trinity needed to be worked out over many years. But these first sermons in Acts repeatedly imply a unique relationship between the two which was to lead to that doctrine. It is the God of the Old Testament who worked mighty works through Jesus. (Acts 2:22.) It is God who raised Jesus from the dead. (Acts 2:24.) It is God whose *Holy One* Jesus is. (Acts 2:27.) And over and over titles are applied to Jesus which in the Old Testament are reserved to God Himself—titles which to Peter and his hearers carried the connotations of deity: "Holy One," "Saviour," "Righteous One," "Judge," and "Lord." Peter does not explicitly call Jesus God. But the Christ whom He has met cannot be described in simply human terms. He bursts the bounds of human categories. In titles and function Jesus is preached as divine. What the God of the Old Testament did for Israel, Jesus was described from the first as doing for the church.

Summary and Conclusions

We have seen in this chapter that:

1. The first preachers preached that Jesus was the promised Messiah of the Old Testament hope, the "Christ," the "Son of David," the "Lord," the Great King.

2. They saw Jesus as the "Prophet like unto Moses," the Hero and Founder of the new people of God.

3. But with a completely new kind of interpretation of the Old Testament, born of the experience of the Resurrection itself, they combined with these ideas other very different Old Testament concepts. Jesus was seen as the Fulfiller of Israel's mission and destiny, in some sense the End and Goal of its ceremonial worship, and to Him were ascribed titles and functions which in the Old Testament were reserved for God.

What does this picture of Jesus, derived from ancient Scriptures, mean for twentieth-century Christians?

First, He is the King. The Lord Jesus has authority. He is, indeed, the Dictator. He comes to men's hearts to rule, or He does not come at all.

Second, He is the Prophet who alone adequately reveals God, who leads the church in the wilderness of this world to a nobler promised land.

Beyond these figures the first sermons remind us that Jesus is the Fulfiller of all that is best in the Old Testament and can be adequately understood only in its light. Priest, ceremony, history, and song all point to Him. We cannot understand Jesus apart from the Old Testament. And, more important, we cannot understand Him apart from the Old Testament God.

One final word of caution: What produced the first sermons was not simply a new interpretation of the Old Testament; it was that the church had met a Man. The center of the preaching was not merely a reinterpretation of Scripture. It was the announcement of an Event. This Man and this Event—Jesus and His life and death, as described in the sermons—form the subject of the next step in our investigation.

CHAPTER 5

JESUS | a Man on Earth

THE NAME "JESUS" did not come into the first preaching through any form of Jewish Messianic expectation, either in the Scripture or in the popular literature of the time. It came through a historical event.

"Jesus is the *Messiah.*" This was the good news proclaimed by the earliest preachers. The statement was equally true and equally important when the emphasis was reversed. "The Messiah is *Jesus.*" Of "the Messiah" everyone had heard for centuries. The new factor was "Jesus."

Yet this new factor was the essential point. The first preachers had as their primary purpose not just the preaching of theories about the nature of the Messiah or new interpretations of Jewish Scripture. The heart of the message was the reporting and interpreting of certain historical facts. Where the old Messianic categories did not fit "Jesus" they were revised, reinterpreted, or sometimes even discarded. The second term, "Jesus," continued essentially unchanged. The gospel was permanently anchored to a historical Person and to historical events.

> . . . the word which was proclaimed throughout all Judea, beginning from Galilee after the baptism which John preached: how God anointed Jesus of Nazareth with the Holy Spirit and with power; how he went about doing good and healing all that were oppressed by the devil, for God was with him. And we are witnesses to all that he did both in the country of the Jews and in Jerusalem.

> They put him to death by hanging him on a tree; but God raised him on the third day . . . (Acts 10:37-40.)

So Peter recounted to Cornelius the earthly life and death of Jesus. Every other recorded sermon found some place for the same story.

In the previous chapters we have examined the contemporary Messianic expectations which the first Christians used to interpret the meaning of the coming of Jesus. In chapter six we shall study the effect of the Resurrection and the exaltation on the first preaching. In this chapter we consider the significance of the report given by the first Christian preachers of the events of the earthly life and death of Jesus of Nazareth, a man on earth.

The Human Nature of Jesus

First we must note Peter's clear presentation of the human nature and origins of Jesus.

At one point the first preaching about Jesus was quite plain: Jesus was *a man.* (Acts 2:22.)

This marks a contrast between Christianity and all its rival religions in the first-century Roman Empire. There were "gods many and lords many" in the pagan cults with which Christianity had to compete. Mythical demigods came to earth in many a heathen legend. But Christianity centered around a real man, a human being, a historical person in a definite place, whose life and death were a matter of public record available to the most sceptical.

It is not clear just what sort of being the Messiah of the Book of Enoch is. He is called "a Son of Man," but he appears to be a kind of super-angel. The first-century world was believed to be filled with angels and demons and every kind of supernatural creature. The first great Christian heresy about the nature of Christ was to be a denial of His humanity. But the first preaching, according to the sermons in Acts, was as clear on this point as the fully developed Nicene Creed. Whatever else He was, Jesus was a *man.*

Even those phrases which indicate His unique relationship to God suggest also a certain distinction from God.

> Jesus of Nazareth, *a man attested* to you *by God* with mighty works and wonders and signs *which God did through Him* in your midst . . . delivered up *according to the* definite *plan and foreknowledge of God,* you crucified . . . But *God raised him up* . . . (Acts 2:22-24.)

Jesus is a man. This man is attested by God, who did great deeds through Him.

> God anointed Jesus of Nazareth with the Holy Spirit and with power . . . for God was with him. (Acts 10:38.)

Jesus is indeed the Spirit-filled agent of God. Yet even so He is a man.

The doctrine of the virgin birth, the doctrine of Christ's coming down from heaven, the doctrine of Jesus as conceived by the Holy Spirit—these doctrines, however clearly seen in later teaching, do not appear explicitly in the recorded sermons of Peter in Acts.

Two titles attest His humanity. One is the proper name, "Jesus." It is true that Matthew's Gospel (1:21) gives this name significance in relation to salvation. But it is not in connection with any previous expectation that the name appears. "Jesus" is a common name, one that appears in the Old Testament in many forms, including the still familiar "Joshua." "*This* Jesus" (Acts 2:23), it is emphasized—for Jesus was a common name—*this* Jesus is the Saviour.

The second title is "the Nazarene." (Acts 2:22.) True, Matthew finds this also to be a fulfillment of Scripture.[1]

But it was scarcely a part of the popular expectation. (John 1:46.) No, it is rather the assertion that Jesus was a man from a real place, Nazareth. (Acts 10:38.) It was the more startling because Nazareth was a town from which nothing good was expected.

Jesus was also preached as being from a certain family. As we have seen,[2] descent from David was a part of the Old Testament Messianic hope; yet Davidic descent placed Jesus squarely within the human framework. He was "of the fruit of his [David's] loins, according to the flesh." (Acts 2:30, K.J.V.) Jesus was a "prophet from your brethren." (Acts 3:22.) His lineage was human.

On this point, then, the thought of the first Christians was as clear as that of those who wrote the Nicene Creed. Jesus was "very man."

His Earthly Life

Few subjects have been more controversial among Biblical scholars than the place of Jesus' earthly life in the earliest Christian thought. Some have felt that the memory of Jesus' words and deeds was the starting point of Christianity. At the opposite extreme, others have maintained that the first Christians forgot Jesus' human existence as they preached His significance, His presence, and His return.

Against the background of this controversy an examination of the sermons in Acts becomes significant. What do these first sermons say about Jesus' earthly life? If we had only these sermons we would know a number of things.

1. Jesus was descended from David and came from the town of Nazareth.

2. He is set in relation to John the Baptist. (Acts 10:37 and 13:25.) The fact that both Peter and Paul are reported

as mentioning this in their preaching suggests that this was a standard part of the *kerygma,* the first preaching. Though Jesus' baptism by John is not explicitly mentioned, this is undoubtedly what is implied. It is related to His being anointed by God "with the Holy Spirit and with power."

The strong influence of the first preaching upon the form of the four Gospels is indicated by the fact that they, too, look upon this baptism by John as the beginning of Jesus' ministry. Indeed, two of the four (Mark and John) tell nothing of Jesus' birth and boyhood but begin their story with the baptism. So Peter speaks of the gospel "word" as "beginning from Galilee after the baptism which John preached." (Acts 10:37.) This baptism was the real beginning of the story. Here Jesus was anointed. Only later, at the Resurrection perhaps, was this anointing publicly proclaimed. So Saul and David were anointed privately to their kingly office, and later publicly acclaimed king. Johannes Weiss, who wrote so much concerning the ideas about Jesus found in the first preaching, believed that originally the disciples thought of Jesus as having become the Messiah at the moment of His baptism.[3]

3. Jesus was seen from the first to be a prophet, one who preached and taught the word of God. (Acts 3:22; 10:36-37.)

What a contrast to the Elect One of the Book of Enoch or to the conquering king of Psalm 110! Jesus from the earliest times was thought of as a prophet, a preacher!

High as their view of Jesus is, the Gospels never forgot that the first preachers had pictured Jesus as a human Teacher.[4]

Yet oddly enough there is scarcely a word in the sermons about the great ethical teachings of our Lord. "Love thy neighbor as thyself" is never quoted. The earliest preaching was about the nature and work of Jesus, not a repetition of what He had said.

This is not to say, however, that Matthew or the church invented teachings and attributed them later to Jesus. From the first His words were regarded as binding. Failure to obey them endangered Israel. (Acts 3:23.) It is to say that the first sermons were more interested in the Teacher than in His teaching. This is the way the first preachers thought of the Great Teacher:

> The Spirit of the Lord God is upon me,
> because the Lord has anointed me
> to bring good tidings to the afflicted;
> he has set me to bind up the brokenhearted,
> to proclaim liberty to the captives,
> and the opening of the prison
> to those who are bound;
> to proclaim the year of the Lord's favor . . .[5]

4. The first sermons told something of the miraculous deeds of Jesus.

Were the miracle stories legends that grew up later, after the actual facts of Jesus' life were forgotten? So some have argued. But our evidence leads to the opposite view. From the beginning, according to the sermons in Acts, preachers told of Jesus as a man attested by God by mighty works, wonders, and signs, which God did through Him among the people, facts which the people themselves were said to know. (Acts 2:22.) The sermon to Cornelius lists healing as a specific example of Jesus' miracles, and it speaks of His works of mercy. (Acts 10:38.) We are told that these miracles began in Galilee and that Jesus also worked in Judea and in Jerusalem, where His ministry ended.

Scholars of the "form-critical" school have shown that our four Gospels are partly composed of stories which were originally used to illustrate the first sermons. Of course the sermons in Acts are greatly condensed. We can imagine the earliest preachers telling story after story to illustrate the ministry of Jesus. One may think of a book like Mark as being partly a collection of sermon illustrations from Peter's preaching about his Lord.[6]

Jesus' life was pictured from the very beginning as an engagement in combat with the devil, accompanied by miracles, healings, and signs. (Acts 10:38.) God's power was revealed in both His words and His deeds. And to these deeds, even as to the Resurrection, the first apostles were witnesses. (Acts 10:39.)

5. The sermons in Acts give us one more thing about the earthly life of Jesus—some intimation of His moral character. He is called, for example, "the Holy and Righteous One," placed in sharp contrast to the murderer Barabbas. (Acts 3:14.)

As "holy," Jesus is pictured as without the blemish of sin, pure, able to stand before God. One may note the cleansing power of His holiness implied in Acts 3:12. The title "Righteous One" implies perfect obedience to God's law. He is so beloved of God (Acts 2:27) that God will not let Him perish. He is God's Servant. (Acts 3:13,26.) And He is in a very special way anointed with the Spirit of God. (Acts 10:38.)

All of these ideas were no doubt expanded by the early preachers so that an inspiring portrait of Jesus' character was a part of every sermon.

The Place and Meaning of Jesus' Life

It thus appears that the earthly life of Jesus was by no means forgotten by the earliest church, even though it also described Him in heavenly terms. From the sermons in Acts alone we could learn of Jesus' human origin—that he was a descendant of David, and that He was from Nazareth. We could learn of His baptism by John as the beginning of His public ministry. We would know that He was a Teacher and Preacher of the Word of God. We would know of His miraculous deeds. And we would know of His holy and righteous character.

However, this memory of Jesus' earthly life as a Holy Teacher was not in conflict with the church's proclamation of Jesus as the divine Lord. Rather His deeds and character were said to show who He was: "Jesus of Nazareth, a man *attested* to you by God *with mighty works* and wonders and signs which God did through him in your midst . . ." (Acts 2:22.)

This word *attested,* or *approved,* is the same as that used by the Jewish historian Josephus in describing the parade by which David attested publicly that his son Solomon would be king. In Jesus' words and deeds His Father was proclaiming the Lordship of the Son. Not only His resurrection but also His earthly life and character showed that "God was with him." (Acts 10:38.)

This is in harmony with Hebrew thought. God, to the Jews, revealed Himself not in philosophy but in "mighty acts." From the first, Jesus' life was seen as the self-revealing mighty act of God.

The Death of Jesus

The fact about the earthly life of Jesus to which the first preachers gave the most attention was His death. Let us look at what the earliest Christians said about the cross.

A crucified Messiah was pleasing neither to Jews nor to Greeks. It might have been expected that the early church would try to conceal or forget the humiliating kind of death which came to its Lord. Exactly the opposite was the case. The cross was the one fact of Jesus' life which every sermon mentioned, the one fact described in greatest detail.[7]

From the sermons we can learn many of the details connected with Jesus' death. The place is given: Jerusalem. Those responsible are named: the Jews, especially their leaders. It is recognized that the Romans carried out the crucifixion, Pilate being specifically named as the official to whom the Jews delivered up Jesus. The Barabbas incident is mentioned, with emphasis on Pilate's readiness to free Jesus and the demand of the crowd that they be given the murderer instead. It is made clear that Jesus is innocent of any crime. The reason given for His death is the ignorance and sin of the people. The manner of His death is described, that He was "hanged on a tree." And it is stated that the Resurrection was on the third day following. All of these facts, except the last, Peter assumes to be widely known.

Now it is more than just a coincidence that the four Gospels exactly parallel this. Just as all four of them begin their account of Jesus' ministry, as do the sermons, with the baptism by John, so all four give in great detail only the story of the death of Jesus. Material concerning the last week of Jesus' life takes up one-fourth to one-half of each of the four Gospels of our New Testament. Only of the last week of Jesus' life have we a day-by-day account of what He did. Indeed, Mark, the oldest Gospel, has been called "a passion [death] narrative with a long introduction." That the first sermons gave far more attention to Jesus' death than to His life fits this picture precisely. Paul can speak of the *kerygma* as "the preaching of the cross."

Professor James S. Stewart lists three things which might

well summarize the interpretation of Jesus' death found in the sermons of Peter in Acts: [8]

First, the cross was man's most flagrant crime. It is made clear that Jesus was the Holy and Righteous One, sharply contrasted with the criminal Barabbas. Yet the ignominy of His death is emphasized by the repeated phrase "hanged on a tree" (reminiscent of Deuteronomy 21:23; compare Galatians 3:13). The blame for the death of Jesus is laid squarely at the feet of Peter's hearers and their leaders. It is pointed out that though they committed the crime in ignorance, God had given them full opportunity to recognize who Jesus was. It is this crime above all, therefore, for which they are urged to repent. The cross is preached until men are "cut to the heart" and cry, "Brethren, what shall we do?" (Acts 2:37.) The cross brings conviction of sin.

Second, behind the apparent tragedy a divine purpose was seen to be at work. Jesus was delivered up "by the determinate counsel and foreknowledge of God." (Acts 2:23, K.J.V.) God's purpose here receives no clear explanation. A fuller understanding was to come later. But Peter is confident that the cross was part of God's plan. Christ's suffering was seen as the fulfillment of that which had been prophesied by all the prophets. (Acts 3:18.)

Third, the death of Christ was connected with the forgiveness of sins. The way in which the cross brings pardon was largely undefined; as to the fact itself, there was never any doubt. At first the connection seems to be one simply of successive experiences. It seems implied that Jesus had to fulfill the prophecies of His suffering, and that now that this has been accomplished the way is clear for the blotting out of sins and the sending of "times of refreshing." (Acts 3:18-19.) Jesus' death was interpreted as a necessary preliminary step toward forgiveness. The fact that Luke does not report these sermons as yet presenting some well-thought-out theory such as the doctrine of the vicarious atonement appears to be another instance of his amazing accuracy. The interpretation of the cross found in Romans, the Corinthian letters, and Hebrews had not yet been developed.

Jesus as the "Servant" of God

If we look in these earliest Christian statements for the origin of later doctrines of atonement one hint can perhaps be found. It lies in the title for Jesus, *Servant* of God. (Acts 3:13, 26.)[9]

In 1 Corinthians 15:3 Paul lists as part of the formula which he himself was taught and which he had taught others, that "Christ died for our sins in accordance with the scriptures." Here, then, in the oldest strata of Christian thought, are discovered three ideas deliberately linked together: the cross, Scripture, and our sins. If, then, we search the sermons of Peter for passages linking these three ideas one possibility is discovered: Peter spoke of the death of Jesus in terms of the "Servant passages" of Isaiah.

"The Servant of the Lord" is a mysterious figure. He is introduced in Isaiah 42:1 with these words:

> Behold my servant, whom I uphold,
> my chosen, in whom my soul delights.

Repeatedly in the second half of Isaiah, poems about this Servant appear.[10] At times he is identified with the nation Israel. (Isaiah 49:3.) At times he appears to be an individual. (Isaiah 53.) Perhaps the most familiar Servant passage is the one which describes how his sacrificial death has brought vicarious atonement to others. (Isaiah 52:13–53:12.)

The New Testament church found Jesus described in

these passages from Isaiah. This is certain. (Acts 8:32-35; Luke 4:17-19.) But did the very first Christians identify Jesus as the Servant? This is a disputed question.

Two reasons have led some scholars to the view that Jesus was not recognized as the Servant by the first Jerusalem Christians. First, it appears that the Jews rarely—probably never—thought of the Messiah as fulfilling Isaiah's prophecy.[11] The Jewish Messiah would be a conqueror, not despised and rejected. Second, Mark, the oldest Gospel, never uses the title "Servant" in connection with Jesus, nor does Paul, first writer of Epistles. No, it is argued, this whole idea would be repugnant to Semitic Christians. Only later Greek thinkers, like Luke, would call Jesus "the Servant of the Lord."

Yet there are reasons to believe that even here the sermons in Acts represent the earliest thought.

First, Semitic literature shows that the religious use of the word "servant" was not uncommon. Semitic priests were proud of names identifying themselves as "servants" of God. The title need not have been repugnant to Jewish Christians.

Second, it may be that Mark was familiar with the identification of Jesus with the figure described in Isaiah. The title "Servant" is not used, it is true, but the language of Isaiah seems to be reflected in several passages in Mark.[12]

Third, there are echoes of Isaiah's "Servant passages" in the writings of Paul. (Romans 4:25.) To what other more likely passage of Scripture can Paul have been referring in his statement that Jesus "died for our sins in accordance with the scriptures"? (1 Corinthians 15:3.) And in Philippians 2:5-11, a passage which many scholars believe to be a quotation from one of the first Christian hymns, originally written in Aramaic, Paul writes that Jesus "emptied himself, taking the form of a *servant* . . . and became obedient unto death . . . " A different word is used for "servant," but the idea is quite the same as that of Isaiah.[13]

Then does the use in Peter's sermons of the title "Servant" for Jesus imply reference to the prophecy of Isaiah? (Acts 3:13,26.) The above investigation of other New Testament books shows no reason to deny this. Moreover, there are strong reasons to think that it does. That Luke himself so understood the term cannot be doubted, in view of Philip's specific identification of Jesus with the figure in Isaiah. (Acts 8:26-40.) Luke professes to have talked with Philip personally. (Acts 21:8.) The title is also used in what may have been a standard formula of prayer in the early church. (Acts 4:27,30.) The use of the title "Servant" in connection with such phrases as "delivered up" and "glorified" (3:13) and "wickedness" (3:26) strongly suggests Isaiah 53. And the anointing of Acts 10:38 is in language suggesting a similar "Servant passage," Isaiah 61:1-3.

There is, therefore, evidence for concluding that from the very first the church identified Jesus with the "Suffering Servant of the Lord" described in Isaiah 53 and similar passages.[14]

If this is true it is a discovery of profound importance. Now we can tell in some detail how the earliest Christians pictured Jesus, and how they found meaning in His death. Verse after verse in Isaiah became for them portraits of the Master. Here is how He was seen by them to have been in His earthly life:

> Behold my servant, whom I uphold,
>   my chosen, in whom my soul delights;
> I have put my spirit upon him,
>   he will bring forth justice to the nations.
> He will not cry or lift up his voice,
>   or make it heard in the street;

a bruised reed he will not break,
and a dimly burning wick he will not quench;
he will faithfully bring forth justice.
He will not fail or be discouraged
till he has established justice in the earth;
and the coastlands wait for his law. (Isaiah 42:1-4.)

He was despised and rejected by men;
a man of sorrows, and acquainted with grief;

. . . .

Surely he has borne our griefs
and carried our sorrows;

. . . .

But he was wounded for our transgressions,
he was bruised for our iniquities;
upon him was the chastisement that made us whole,
and with his stripes we are healed.
All we like sheep have gone astray;
we have turned every one to his own way;
and the Lord has laid on him
the iniquity of us all. (Isaiah 53: 3-6.)

Reading such passages the reader almost hears the voice from the burning bush saying, "Put off your shoes from your feet, for the place on which you are standing is holy ground." (Exodus 3:5.) For if our conclusion is right, this is how the earliest Christians pictured Jesus. This is how they described His earthly life and how they explained the meaning of His death. It was a long way from a logically developed theory of the atonement, but it was an inspired start! From this beginning great doctrines would come.

Conclusions

In this chapter we have studied what the first preachers said about the events of the earthly life and death of Jesus.

This study points to three facts as important for understanding Jesus in the twentieth century as in the first:

1. Jesus was a real man. Thus Christianity is based not simply on legends, myths, philosophies, or dreams but on the interpretation of actual historical events. Pagan religions might be founded on theories and visions. From the very beginning Christianity has centered its thought on a real man. Sceptics may question the Christian interpretation of this man. But His life in a real time and His death at a real place are historic facts.

2. From the beginning the words, deeds, and character of this man were regarded as showing His unique relationship to God. Those scholars are wrong who have supposed that interest in Jesus' earthly life grew up only among the second generation of Christians. On the other hand, scholars are also wrong who have supposed that Christianity began with simple admiration for a human hero. What we have found is that from the first, Christian preachers told stories of the mighty deeds of the Great Teacher as signs that in a special sense God was with Him.

3. The cross has always been the most important fact of Jesus' earthly life. We find that it is not a case of later Christians endeavoring to explain or apologize for an embarrassing fact they could not hide. From the first the story of Jesus' death was proclaimed in every sermon. No well-thought-out theory of its meaning appears in the beginning, though there are strong hints that Jesus is connected with the vicariously suffering Servant of Isaiah. But from the first, Jesus' death was somehow known to be essential to our salvation.

CHAPTER 6

JESUS | the Risen and Exalted One

WHAT, IN THE EARLIEST PICTURE OF JESUS, was in greatest contrast to all later ideas about Him? What most distinguishes the first preachers' thought about Jesus from the view of Him in the rest of the New Testament? Is it not their unique emphasis on and interpretation of the exaltation of Jesus, the change in His status which accompanied the Resurrection?

By the time of the writing of the Gospel According to John it was possible to think of Jesus' life before the Resurrection in a very different way, to see in every word and deed of Jesus the revelation of the glory of God that was indeed there. But in the days closest to the events of the cross and the Resurrection, the consciousness of the contrast between the shame and the glory of Jesus was still vivid. The Good News was of the transformation that began at Easter. Jesus had been raised to a completely new and unexpected status. What His mighty works had hinted was now made clear. He who had once lived humbly as a man among men, who had been a Servant, who had suffered the most ignominous death —this One had now suddenly been exalted to the right hand of God and had been made by God "both Lord and Christ." The first proclamation was:

> Let all the house of Israel therefore know assuredly that God has made him both Lord and Christ, this Jesus whom you crucified. (Acts 2:36.)

Of this unexpected change the Resurrection was the sign.

"Thus the verdict of man was reversed by the verdict of God." [1] But there was more than a verdict here. God had actually raised Jesus to an entirely new position. "God exalted him at his right hand as Leader and Savior." (Acts 5:31.) The Suffering Servant, whom men had shamefully killed, was now raised by God and exalted to His right hand in heaven as Triumphant Lord.

So pronounced is this sense of contrast that some have even argued that the first doctrine of Jesus' nature was really this: Jesus during His earthly life was a man, but at His death He was made the Son of God. Of the truth and falsehood of this interesting proposal we shall be better prepared to speak at the end of the chapter.

The Importance of the Resurrection

Some have imagined that the story of the resurrection of Christ was a legend which grew up over the years after His death. Many a twentieth-century sceptic has supposed that the memory of the good man, Jesus, gradually grew into the myth of the risen god. The story of the Resurrection is called a late afterthought.

This view is shattered on the cold facts of research. If the sermons in Acts do reflect the earliest thoughts about Jesus, then from the very beginning the resurrection and exaltation of Jesus were an essential part of the preaching. In fact, the further back we can probe, the more important the Resurrection seems to have been.

Every sermon attributed to Peter proclaims it. Here is the kind of thing the first preachers said, over and over:

> This Jesus God raised up, and of that we all are witnesses. Being therefore exalted at the right hand of God... (Acts 2:32-33.)

> [You] killed the Author of life, whom God raised from the dead. (Acts 3:15.)

> The God of our fathers raised Jesus whom you killed by hanging him on a tree. God exalted him at his right hand as Leader and Savior. (Acts 5:30-31.)

> They put him to death by hanging him on a tree; but God raised him on the third day. (Acts 10:39-40.)

So central was this message that Peter can describe himself and the other apostles simply as witnesses to the Resurrection. (Acts 2:32; 3:15; compare 1:22.) This was no late sentimental addition. It was the central fact of the original gospel.

That Luke was accurate in so reporting the first preaching is substantiated by a careful study of the rest of the New Testament. Romans 10:9 makes witness to the Resurrection a part of the earliest confession of faith. The very phrases of this confession are echoed throughout the Epistles.[2] C. H. Dodd has shown how nearly every passage in the Epistles which seems to reflect the earliest preaching speaks of the Resurrection.[3] Even more significant is the clear fact that not a line of the New Testament was written by anyone who did not believe in the Resurrection. Always, from the oldest material to the latest, this is essential, and the older the writing the more important the place given the Resurrection.

The Nature of the Resurrection

A much more difficult question, however, is this: How did the first Christians conceive of the Resurrection? Was it the reanimation of a physical body, a series of mystic visions, a conviction of Jesus' immortality, or what?

In so far as as we can learn from the sermons in Acts, the

first Christians proclaimed the resurrection of Christ as unmistakably real, even materially real. Peter, in connection with the Resurrection, quotes from Psalm 16, "Thou wilt not . . . let thy Holy One see corruption." (Acts 2:27.) This quotation suggests the conservation of the very same body that was put in the grave. The Resurrection is described in surprisingly physical terms.

Thus we are told that the Resurrection occurred on a particular day, the third. (Acts 10:40.) The risen Jesus is seen by the apostles. He gives them commands. He even eats and drinks with these disciples. It is true that only a few individuals are named as having seen the Risen Christ, but this is explained in terms of the fact that only believers were witnesses of the Resurrection. There is no suggestion that the experience was not material.

It is interesting that, unlike the account in Luke's own Gospel, the story of the women at the tomb is not even mentioned in Acts, and the emphasis is laid entirely on collective experiences of the apostles. In this respect the sermons are like the account which Paul says he received when he first became a Christian. (1 Corinthians 15:3-7.)

Some have argued that this idea of the physical resurrection of Jesus must have been a later development. The picture of Jesus eating and drinking with His disciples after the Resurrection, for example, suggests details added by a later storyteller to embellish his narrative. Yet it may be said in defense of the account in Acts that this materialistic concept of the Resurrection seems more at home among the Jews of the Jerusalem church than among the more sophisticated Greeks of the church of a few years later. It was the Greeks who had sharply distinguished soul from body and taught the immortality of the soul. It was not the preaching of a hero's immortality or of visions and myths from the heavenly realm which repelled the Greeks at Athens. (Acts 17:32.) They were familiar enough with these ideas. Nor were such stories sufficiently novel in Palestine to start a movement comparable to the Christian church. It was the startling message of the actual resurrection of a real man which produced these reactions.

Therefore, in so far as the sermons in Acts give information, it must be concluded that the first preachers believed in a "bodily" resurrection. It was not simply visions of an immortal spirit but the revivification of a physical body which these sermons described.

Although traces of this almost crude Hebrew concept of bodily resurrection are clearly seen in the sermons in Acts, this is not the whole picture. The first preachers also saw the Resurrection as a cosmic event of the highest spiritual significance. This meaning must now be examined.

The Meaning of the Resurrection

How did the first Christians interpret the Resurrection? What did they see as its spiritual meaning?

First, the Resurrection was regarded as the event which vindicated Jesus' ministry. By it, God reversed the decision of man. The Jews had delivered up Jesus to Pilate to be crucified, a most shameful death, and had demanded a murderer in preference to Him. But by the Resurrection, God made it clear that Jesus was God's Servant, the Holy and Just One. It is the Resurrection vindication which Scripture foretold. (Acts 4:10-11.) By this event the true character of Jesus' earthly ministry was revealed. The news of the Resurrection caused men to be "cut to the heart" (Acts 2:37) with a new realization of what they had done.

The Resurrection, however, was interpreted as announcing more than just what Jesus *was*. It showed what Jesus now *is*—His new status, His exaltation to the right hand of God. In what may well be a quotation from a commonly accepted early creed, Paul writes that Jesus was "declared to be the Son of God with power . . . by the resurrection from the dead." (Roman 1:4, K.J.V.) This thought is parallel to that of the sermons in Acts.

In this sense the Resurrection is the proof that Jesus' exaltation has taken place. Only after he has described the Resurrection can Peter announce, "Let all the house of Israel therefore know assuredly that God has made him both Lord and Christ . . ." (Acts 2:36.) It is the Resurrection which guarantees this fact. It was only through this event that the apostles received the command to preach Jesus in His new office as Cosmic Judge of the living and the dead. (Acts 10:42.)

Thus, whatever the nature of the Resurrection experiences, they represented to the disciples far more than the reanimation of Jesus' body. It was the Resurrection which demonstrated to them conclusively that Jesus was exalted to the right hand of God, that the new age had begun. "Prince," "Saviour," "Lord," "Christ," "Judge"—all these are titles derived primarily not from the virgin birth or the perfect life but from the Resurrection.

The Resurrection was more than the *proof* of the exaltation of Jesus to God's right hand; it was seen as the *means* by which this had been accomplished. "Exaltation" and "Resurrection" are not clearly distinguished; the one seems the inevitable accompaniment of the other. (Acts 2:32-33.) The two terms are in a sense synonymous. The Resurrection appearances are that aspect of the event which can be described. The exaltation is never described. That Jesus had been exalted to God's right hand can only be triumphantly affirmed. But this exaltation—not the reanimation of a dead body, like that of Lazarus—is the message. Jesus has been exalted to the right hand of God.

Exaltation to the "Right Hand of God"

Modern preachers speak a great deal of Jesus' resurrection. The first preachers spoke as often of His exaltation "to the right hand of God." [4] This curious phrase implies three things:

First, "the right hand of God" is not a matter of location but of honor. The Jews did not think of God as confined to a physical body with hands and feet but recognized that He fills all creation. Rather, the phrase is a sign of supreme divine honor bestowed upon Jesus. Jewish rabbis were accustomed to say that God had created the earth with His left hand, but with His right hand He had created the heavens. He who sits at the right hand of God on the throne is no longer Servant. He is Co-ruler.

Second, "at the right hand of God" implies a certain distinction from God. The figure of speech precludes the idea of absorption into the One who occupies the throne. The distinction of Persons in the Godhead found in the creeds preserves this separation.

Third, the phrase implies a certain equality with God. Titles once applied to God alone are now applied to Jesus. Functions thought exclusively divine are ascribed to Him. Jesus now pours out the Holy Spirit. He bestows forgiveness. Thus Jesus stands in a relationship to the believer comparable only to that of God Himself.

This "exaltation" is not simply Jesus' ascension. It is something more basic than that, of a more spiritual nature. It is interesting to note the difference here between the sermons and Luke's own viewpoint. Only Luke gives in detail the account of Jesus' bodily ascension into heaven. (Acts 1.) For Luke the story seems to have as its primary significance the termination of Jesus' ministry in the flesh. But the "exaltation" in the sermons is a transformation of status, from Servant to Lord. By exalting Him "God has made him both Lord and Christ." (Acts 2:36.)

Incarnation Versus Adoption

The unique emphasis on the exaltation of Jesus found in the sermons in Acts has led some scholars to conclude that the earliest Christians thought of Jesus as having been born a man but having been "adopted" at His resurrection as the Son of God.

Orthodox Christianity has always affirmed that in the Person of Jesus, God became man. "The Word was God . . . and the Word became flesh and dwelt among us . . . " (John 1:1, 14.) Is it possible that one may discover in the sermons in Acts traces of an earlier doctrine? Did Christians at first fail to understand how God had become a man and preach rather of a man who had been exalted to become God?

The continental scholar Paul Wernle implies that the doctrine of the nature of Christ evolved backward, as it were.[5] At first, Jesus was thought of as a man who would become Messiah when He should come to judge and to save at the end of time. Later, according to Wernle, Jesus was conceived of as being made Lord and Christ at the Resurrection. Still later it was said that Jesus was adopted as the Son of God at His baptism, as indicated by the voice which said, "Thou art my beloved Son." (Found in the earliest Gospel, Mark 1:11.) At a still later stage, according to this view, men learned the story of Jesus' being conceived by the Holy Spirit and born of the Virgin Mary, as told in the later Gospels of Matthew and Luke (though not mentioned by Mark—or by Paul). And finally, said Wernle, the Fourth Gospel pictured Jesus as pre-existent. ("In the beginning was the Word . . ." John 1:1.) So the understanding of the church developed, finding signs of Jesus' divinity earlier and earlier in His career.

However, one must be very cautious, even sceptical, here. The above evolutionary theory is much too simple and "logical" to fit all the facts. For example, Paul, though the earliest New Testament writer and one who never mentions Jesus' virgin birth, clearly taught Jesus' pre-existence. (Colossians 1:15-17.) And the earliest sermons, recorded in Acts, do not fit precisely this pattern of evolution.

It is impossible to find a consistent pronouncement in these sermons that Jesus became the Christ at one certain stage in His ministry. Acts 10:37-38 seems, like Mark, to suggest that Jesus became the Christ at His baptism. Acts 2:36 seems to represent Jesus as becoming Christ at His resurrection. The suggestion that Jesus was "adopted" at His baptism but not proclaimed till His resurrection does not fit with the assertion of Acts 2:22 that His mighty works during His earthly life also proclaimed Him to be the Christ.[6] Luke himself, of course, believed that Jesus was conceived by the Holy Ghost. (Luke 1:26-38.) Finally, the first preachers seem to have identified Jesus with Enoch's "Son of Man," who was pre-existent.[7]

Actually, what Acts carefully records is the groping of the earliest Christians for forms to express their experience, their earliest discoveries of new and sometimes seemingly conflicting meanings in glorious events. It was not a time of simple, consistent, clear theological reasoning. It was a time of ecstatic utterance of truths not yet fully understood.

There are great differences between the exaltation of Jesus and the legend about Hercules.[8] The Greek hero was said to have been carried at the last moment to heaven, there to become a sort of god. But in the pagan story Hercules accomplished no saving death and resurrection, there is involved no glorious vindication, and Hercules is lifted to no place in the Greek pantheon comparable to the place of Christ. His story belongs to the realm of myth. Whatever else Jesus was, everyone knew that He was a real, historical person.

Most important of all, what is said of Jesus is not that His *nature* was changed, from human to divine, but that His *status* was changed, from Suffering Servant to reigning Lord. Messiahship was a matter of office and function, not of inherent nature. Jesus was anointed for a mission; He was raised to new glory. But it is never said that He was at any time any the less human or any more divine.

Conclusions

It is impossible to exaggerate the importance of the Resurrection for Christianity. The Apostle Paul, recalling what he himself had been taught when he first became a Christian, says frankly that if the Resurrection has not actually occurred the whole of the Christian faith falls to the ground. (1 Corinthians 15:3,17.) If the Resurrection is false, Christianity itself is futile. Therefore there is no subject of historical research more important for the modern Christian than the earliest accounts of the Resurrection. Our study of what the first preachers said about the Resurrection reveals three facts:

1. Research cannot discover a time when Christians did not preach the Resurrection as supremely important. The

unbeliever may suppose that the story of the Resurrection was a legend which gradually grew up over the years to give a happy ending to the tragic story of Jesus' life and death. Careful research, however, shows such a view to be absolutely false. The closer one gets to the event the more important the Resurrection becomes.

2. The earliest witnesses of the Resurrection described it in terms of actual fact. The sermons in Acts do not report myths, dreams, or theories about the immortality of the soul. The Christian faith rests upon a historic event, witnessed by men as having happened in a real place at a real time—an event which could be described sometimes in crudely materialistic terms.

3. The importance of the Resurrection, however, lies not in the physical miracle so much as in what this miracle means. The modern Christian quite misses the point of the Resurrection story if he thinks of it simply as the account of a phenomenal event of 2,000 years ago. The importance of the Resurrection lies in what it tells about Jesus. It was the proof and the means of Jesus' exaltation. By it Jesus was triumphantly vindicated and raised to the right hand of God. By it men know and can come into present experience of Jesus as the living, all-powerful Lord.

"God exalted him at his right hand as Leader and Savior, to give repentance to Israel and forgiveness of sins." (Acts 5:31.)

CHAPTER 7

JESUS a Living and Present Power

WHAT DID JESUS MEAN PERSONALLY to a member of the Jerusalem church? Granted that he looked forward to Jesus' coming as Judge, back to Jesus as a man on earth, and up to Jesus as the Exalted One, what did Jesus mean for a Christian continually, in his daily life?

The sermons in Acts picture Jesus as a living and present Power. By His exaltation Jesus was lifted above men to a position of equality with God. This, however, did not make Him unapproachable through worship. And, of special importance, it did not limit Jesus' approach to His disciples. The very fact that He was now at the right hand of God gave Jesus all the more access to men and all the more power with which to help them.

The salvation given by Jesus was not simply a gift bestowed in the past at Calvary, or a hope for the end of the world; it was a present experience. Jesus was present daily with His church; He was their living Saviour and Lord, bestowing upon them now the gifts of forgiveness and the Holy Spirit. Let us see how the first preachers described Jesus as a living and present Power.

Jesus and the Holy Spirit

First, Jesus is related to the Holy Spirit, now transforming men's lives.

It is probably true that Peter never heard of a "doctrine

of the Trinity." The formula of later creeds—that God is in three persons, Father, Son, and Holy Spirit; and these three are "one God, the same in substance, equal in power and glory" [1]—was a wonderfully logical statement, but it came from a much later time. Indeed, the word "Trinity" never occurs in Scripture. It took years of theological discussion to work out this understanding.

What Peter preached was the theology of an ecstasy, not the conclusion of a council of theologians. He knew that something dynamic and revolutionary was happening to men, and he knew that the source of this experience was Jesus Christ. For Peter, Jesus is the One who is now pouring forth on earth the transforming Spirit of God. (Acts 2:33.)

All that Jesus had been and continued to be resulted from His own relationship to the Holy Spirit of God, for "God anointed Jesus of Nazareth with the Holy Spirit and with power." (Acts 10:38.) Empowered by this Spirit He healed, cast out devils, died for man's sins, and was raised and exalted in triumph.

Now Jesus, in fulfillment of Joel's prophecy (Acts 2:16-21), pours out this same Spirit upon young and old. He offers the Holy Spirit to all. (Acts 2:38; 5:32.) "Be baptized . . . and you shall receive the gift of the Holy Spirit." The Spirit is His power, now operative in the Christian fellowship for life, love, strength, and witnessing. Through the Spirit, Jesus was present in all the joy and power of His exaltation for those who were baptized in His name.

The "Name"

The Messiah had not yet been fully revealed in all His triumph over Satan as He would be at the end of the age, but His *name* had been revealed. This was a fact of tremendous importance for the Hebrew, to whom names had meaning and power.

The twentieth-century Christian who wishes to understand first-century Christian thought should know something of this ancient Oriental concept of "the name."

Even today there is a legend told in the East to explain the appearance of disdain for man attributed to the haughty camel. Allah has a hundred names, it is said. Man knows ninety-nine of these, but the other is known only to the camel!

The Old Testament abounds in illustrations of the concept of "the name." To get another's name is to have a certain control over him. Thus the Wrestler demanded of Jacob his name. (Genesis 32:27.) Jacob was changed in some sense as he was given the new name "Israel." Names are revelations of character. God revealed Himself to Moses by telling him His name. (Exodus 3:13-15; 6:2-6.) All through the Old Testament, salvation is "in the name of the Lord," for those who "call upon His name." For the *name* is the revealed nature and the available power of the Divine.

It is striking that what was in the Old Testament exclusively associated with God (salvation through the name) is now applied to Jesus. For the earliest Christians, "Jesus" was the new and powerful saving *name*.

The Name appears in four associations in the sermons of Peter.

First, there is the phrase "faith in his name." (Acts 3:16.) Here "the Name" is the object of trust and devotion. Indeed, the occasion of the whole sermon in Acts 3 is to announce that it is faith in the Name which has brought healing.

Second, the Name is associated with healing. (Acts 3:16; 4:10.) As in Acts 2 the power of the Spirit is said to be manifested by speaking with tongues and prophecy, so in Acts 3 the power of the Name is manifested by active deeds. It was not any power of the disciples which healed the lame man. It was the power of Jesus' name. The idea of healing through a name seems curious and magical in the twentieth century. It is true to the thought of the first. When Jesus' disciples protested that one not of their number was casting out devils in Jesus' name there is no surprise that the use of this name was effective. The only objection was to its unauthorized use. (Mark 9:38.) A second-century synagogue ruling forbade the use of the name of Jesus to cast out devils or to heal. "It was effective, but it was wrong." [2] Jesus was still for the early church the Great Physician.

A third association of "the Name" is with baptism. (Acts 2:38.) Here again one feels Luke's accuracy as a historian. Clearly, baptism was the custom of the Christian church from the beginning. John 4:1-2 even states that the custom began before Jesus' death. Certainly it would appear that Paul was baptized, probably as early as A.D. 33. (1 Corinthians 12:13; compare Acts 9:18.) His Epistles presuppose the practice as universal in the church and associate baptism with the name of Jesus. (1 Corinthians 12:13; 1:13; 6:11.)

Fourth, the Name is associated with forgiveness and salvation. Baptism in the name of Jesus is the sign of this forgiveness. "There is no other name under heaven given among men by which we must be saved." (Acts 4:12.)

Jesus as Saviour

The good news about Jesus is that He is the *Saviour* of the world. In this, too, Jesus is a present Power.

The title *Saviour* is used only once, but that Jesus brings salvation is the promise of every sermon.

> . . . there is salvation in no one else . . . (Acts 4:12.)
>
> God exalted him at his right hand as Leader and Savior, to give repentance to Israel and forgiveness of sins. (Acts 5:31.)
>
> . . . every one who believes in him receives forgiveness of sins through his name. (Acts 10:43.)

It was this promise which attracted men and women to the new faith by the thousands, from every part of the Roman world.

What did the first preachers mean when they called Jesus "Saviour" and promised salvation through Him?

There was a future, heavenly salvation to be received at the final judgment. Jesus was thought of as the divinely appointed Judge, about to visit God's judgment upon mankind. Those saved through faith and baptism would be among the elect group allowed to enter His Messianic kingdom in that day.

Jesus, however, was not thought of as Saviour only at the future judgment. In four ways He is pictured as being also the Saviour here and now.

First, the gift of the Holy Spirit in healing and witnessing power is part of this salvation.

Second, Jesus has brought a present turning of Israel from her sins. He has already begun and is now engaged in the task of giving repentance to the Jews and purifying the chosen people. (Acts 3:26; 5:31.) Jesus has brought a new revelation of God's will which includes an immediate demand for new obedience and a new power to help the Christian obey.

Third, forgiveness is in part a present experience. (Acts 2:38; 5:31.) Assurance of pardon comes now, with faith and baptism, not simply at a future judgment day. If the sermons in Acts are accurate in their report of the first preaching, then the doctrine of justification by faith was not an invention of Paul. He simply worked out logically what was implied in the earliest preaching.[3]

Finally, Jesus was the Saviour of men in this life because He brought them into the new covenant community of God's elect people here and now. For this fellowship He was *Author, Pioneer,* and *Prince.* (Acts 3:15; 5:31.) He was already the church's *Saviour,* and He was already the church's *Lord.*

Lord of the Church

The picture of Jesus as the personal Lord of the chosen company of His followers is of such importance that it must be carefully examined.

The word *church* is not used in the sermons of Peter, perhaps because they come from a time before that word was common. But entrance into the community related to Jesus is clearly offered:

> For to you is the promise, and to your children, and to all that are afar off, even as many as the Lord our God shall call unto him. (Acts 2:39, A.S.V.; compare Isaiah 44:3 and Acts 3:25.)

For this elect fellowship He is *Captain* [4] (Acts 3:15; 5:31), the New Joshua, Pioneer Leader of God's people, the Second Moses, establishing and ruling the covenant congregation. And over and over, in language suggesting Psalm 110, Jesus is called *Lord.*

The idea that Jesus was *Lord* of a company of believers may have been of great importance in the spread of the gospel in the Roman Empire. There were in the ancient world, as Paul tells us, "many gods and many lords." (1 Corinthians

8:5.) The weird, exotic mystery cults of the time believed in the existence of many gods. A particular cult often had in addition its own special *lord*. He was more intimately related to the believers, their special saviour, their personal helper in trouble. For example, an early competitor of Christianity for the faith of the ancient world was the religion of Mithra, originating in the East but soon widespread, especially in the Roman army. Its adherents believed in the existence of many gods, but the special *lord* of the group was Mithra, to whom they related themselves by mystic ceremonies somewhat comparable to baptism and communion. For Christians, Jesus was One Divine *Lord,* better than any pagan cult could offer.

Followers of Jesus were related to Him by faith (Acts 3:16) and by baptism in His name (Acts 2:38). They owed Him absolute obedience. (Acts 3:22.) And though this covenant community was thought of at first primarily in terms of the Hebrews, there were already suggestions that it was broader than one race. (Acts 3:25.) Its bounds were set by the Holy Spirit and the One who calls. (Acts 2:39.) For His followers Jesus is already Pioneer and Prince of Life (Acts 3:15), who, having gone before them into death, has conquered the enemy. He has now established and begun to reign over the Resurrection community.

How Jesus was personal *Lord* of the Christian is illustrated by this fact: The Aramaic word for "Lord," *Maran,* was never used except in compounds such as with "my" or "our." (See 1 Corinthians 16:22.) Jesus was not called in Aramaic *the* Lord, but *my* Lord or *our* Lord. His reign was a personal one over persons. He possessed them and they possessed Him.

Jesus can make absolute demands upon His followers. The apostles have now but one purpose in life, to serve their

Lord. They are His witnesses, the heralds of the King. This is the reason for the preaching. (Acts 10:42.)

Two Conclusions

Speaking with tongues and casting out demons through the *Name* may at first seem to be outmoded ideas to modern Christians. But the earliest preaching of Jesus as a living and present Power has a double message for Christians in every age:

1. Faith in Jesus is based on continuing personal experience. The believer knows who Jesus is because he meets Jesus daily through the Spirit.

This is not to discount the importance of the Bible. Without the witness of Peter and John and the others we would never even have heard of Jesus. Their writings are a necessary guide to our understanding of Him, an essential check against the misunderstandings to which sinful men are prone.

It is to say, however, that faith in Jesus becomes a first-hand experience. The modern Christian is not completely dependent upon historical research for his knowledge of Jesus, as he is for his knowledge of Caesar. According to the first preachers Jesus is still alive, and men may meet Him and see what He is doing today. Faith in Jesus, then, does not stand or fall with the historical accuracy of every word of the New Testament. Through baptism, through repentance, through faith, through the fellowship of the church, men still meet Jesus. And in the Spirit, men learn for themselves personally who our Lord and Saviour is.

2. From the beginning Jesus has stood in a relationship to His followers comparable only to that of God.

Jesus was from the beginning called quite clearly "a

man." Even in His exaltation He was distinguished from God. We have had to note, however, from time to time how often titles and functions which formerly were ascribed to God are now ascribed to Jesus. In the Old Testament it is God who is Lord, Judge, and Saviour. It is He who pours out the Spirit upon men. It is in His name that men are saved. It is He alone who can forgive sins. He alone rules over the covenant people. He only can command with absolute authority. To Him alone is worship to be given. Neither emperor nor angel nor pagan deity could ever take God's place for the Jew. But all of these functions are now ascribed to Jesus.

> . . . we do not appreciate truly the place of Christ in the apostles' faith until we see that where salvation is concerned He stands upon God's side, confronting men . . . There can be no doubt that . . . Peter looks upon Jesus in His exaltation as forming with God His Father one Divine causality at work through the Spirit for the salvation of men . . . His relation to those experiences which constitute Christian life is that of being their Author, the Divine Source from which they come; He is not to Christian faith a Christian, but all Christians owe their being, as such, to Him.[5]

Did the first Christians believe that Jesus was God? The sermons in Acts do not call Him by that name. Working out the doctrines of the incarnation and the Trinity may have required thinkers like Paul and the experience of generations in the church. But historical research cannot discover a time, even the earliest time, when Jesus did not stand in a relationship to the church comparable only to that of God Himself.

CHAPTER 8

JESUS | in the Preaching of Stephen

ONE OF THE STRANGEST and possibly one of the oldest passages in all the New Testament is the sermon attributed to Stephen and found in Acts 7.

Thus far we have been dealing with the sermons in Acts attributed to Peter. In this chapter we shall examine Stephen's address and seek to find what light it sheds on the earliest ideas about Jesus.

The Interpretation of Stephen's Address

Generations of commentators have been puzzled by the seventh chapter of Acts. John Calvin commented, "Stephen's reply at first seems absurd and inept." Another great scholar of Reformation days, Erasmus, said of it, "Many things in this speech have not very much pertinency to the matter which Stephen undertook." Indeed, a modern commentator boldly suggests that Luke himself did not understand it.

All kinds of questions arise. Why is this address so very long? It is out of all proportion to the rest of the book. Luke was too polished a writer to include so long a speech in so short and selective a work as Acts without reason. Yet he records no other speech of similar length, even from the lips of Jesus Himself, in his Gospel or in Acts.

Why is the address not better related to the charges brought against Stephen in the narrative? Erasmus' comment that much of what Stephen says seems to have little bearing on the situation Luke describes appears, at first, quite true.

Just what is this speech all about? Why do we have recorded this seemingly wandering discourse about Abraham in Mesopotamia, Joseph in Egypt, the beauty of Moses, and the tabernacle's priority to the temple? Is it possible that Luke himself did not understand it all?

These very problems suggest one strong possibility: Luke is here preserving for us some written document which he believed to contain the very words of Stephen himself.[1] The address is disproportionately long because it is given to us as Luke found it. It is poorly related to its context because it is not by the author of the story in which it now lies. It has a strange, allegorical style, in contrast to Luke's polished, straightforward Greek, because these words were really spoken by a Hellenistic Jewish rabbi. There is, therefore, reason to believe that Acts 7 goes back to some very early report of the words of the first Christian martyr.

Why was this document so important that it was thus preserved? A very possible answer is this: There are strong hints that it was Stephen who was the father of Christian missions! [2]

The Gospels and Acts both trace the command to preach to all nations back to the lips of the Risen Christ; but it is clear that in the earliest years the church ignored this obligation. Peter's sermons are presented to us as those of a Jewish Christian to Jews (except Cornelius) in the Jewish homeland. His sermons thus represent the earliest stage of the Christian preaching.

But Stephen is a Hellenist; that is, a Jew from outside Palestine. He bears a Greek name. He first appears as one chosen to heal the strife between Hellenists and Jews. (Acts 6:1-5.) And it is among foreign Jews that he speaks. (Acts

6:9.) Add to this the similarity in his treatment of the Old Testament to that of the Alexandrian Jewish teacher of the same era, Philo, and other Hellenists, and the picture of Stephen as a man of broad culture and outlook becomes even clearer.

These considerations lend point to the statement in Acts that at the death of Stephen

> a great persecution arose against the church in Jerusalem; and they were all scattered throughout the region of Judea and Samaria, except the apostles. . . . Now those who were scattered went about preaching the word. (Acts 8:1,4.)

With the martyrdom of Stephen the Christian missionary program, at least to Samaritans and foreign Jews, began. It is true that the apostles remained in Jerusalem, but the Greek followers of Stephen—men with Greek names like Philip—began to spread the gospel beyond the Holy Land. It is no accident that it is in connection with Stephen that we first meet the greatest Christian missionary, Paul.

We have, then, two keys with which to unlock the door to the mysteries of this curious address: First, Stephen is a Hellenistic Jew and may be expected to use the style of Jewish teachers in Alexandria and elsewhere who found in the Old Testament types and allegories to illustrate their points; and second, he is a man whose consciousness of the transcendence of Christ paved the way for the Christian world mission.

Three themes recur in Stephen's address: (1) The law is something added to the covenant promise, which came long before the Jewish law. (2) God is not confined to a holy land or a holy temple. And (3) the Jews have always rejected their saviours. These themes are not discussed in order one after another but are intertwined on the thread of sacred history. It was this preaching of a Christ above law, land, temple, or race that brought Stephen to his death, and the church to its mission.

What does this ancient document tell about the earliest beliefs concerning Jesus? Let us look at Stephen's sermon in Acts 7 in the light of the five ideas about Jesus found in the sermons of Peter.

Jesus as the Transcendent Messiah

Stephen, like Peter but going beyond Peter, sees Jesus as the hoped-for Cosmic Judge of the nations, the One who has ushered in the last age.

It is a point which many overlook that the climax of Stephen's address, the thing which finally brings the enraged mob to lynch him, is not an attack on the Jewish race, or the temple, or the law. It is his proclamation of Jesus Christ as the "Son of man." (Acts 7:52,56.)

It is highly significant that the phrase "Son of man," used here by Stephen, occurs nowhere else in the New Testament except on the lips of Jesus Himself. "Son of man" seems to have been Jesus' favorite designation of Himself. The disciples, however, never are pictured as using it of Him, and it is never again used in the New Testament except in Stephen's address. The simplest explanation for this fact is that the phrase was not understood outside Palestine and thus was used only in the earliest period of Christian thought, the days of the Jerusalem church.

What does the phrase "Son of man" mean? Students differ on the meaning of the title as Jesus Himself used it. Perhaps sometimes He used it to relate Himself in humble love to mankind, reflecting its use in the prophets. (Ezekiel 2:1, 3,6, etc.; Jeremiah 50:40; 51:43; compare Luke 19:10.) Perhaps for Jesus it also connoted the Heavenly Judge. (Matthew 25:31.)

It is clearly in this latter sense that Stephen used the term: "Behold, I see the heavens opened, and the Son of man standing at the right hand of God." (Acts 7:56.) It is the Cosmic Christ whom Stephen sees.

This places us once again squarely in the world of the Jewish hope of the coming Judge. Enoch calls the angelic figure he describes as standing before God not only "the Righteous One" (Acts 7:52) but also "the Son of man" (Acts 7:56; compare Enoch 46:1-6).

Behind Enoch, indeed, the title goes back to the book of Daniel.[3] Here is the strange dream of that ancient seer:

> I saw in the night visions,
>
> and behold, with the clouds of heaven
> there came one like a *son of man*,
> and he came to the Ancient of Days
> and was presented before him.
> And to him was given dominion
> and glory and kingdom,
> *that all peoples, nations, and languages*
> *should serve him;*
> his dominion is an everlasting dominion,
> which shall not pass away,
> and his kingdom one
> that shall not be destroyed.
> (Daniel 7:13-14.)

Note carefully the words in italics above: "All peoples, nations, and languages should serve him," the Son of man.

Is it not possible that this is the solution to the mystery of Stephen? He it was who saw Jesus as the heavenly "Son of man" whom *all* peoples, nations, and languages should serve. Stephen's concept of Jesus' transcending the Jewish land and people suggests why, though other Christian leaders had been imprisoned and beaten, it was Stephen who was the first to be killed. This is why the Christian world mission began with him. It was Stephen who first preached in its universal significance the revolutionary idea of Jesus as the "Son of man."

Much of what at first seems irrelevant in Stephen's address is now seen to bear witnesses to the transcendence of Jesus. His intertwined comments on Jewish law, land, and temple spring from Stephen's conviction that the Son of man is for all peoples.

Jesus is above the Holy Land. Hence Stephen points out in his narrative of Old Testament history that God revealed Himself in Mesopotamia (Acts 7:2), in Egypt (Acts 7:9), and in the wilderness (Acts 7:30). The God of the "Son of man" cannot be confined to Palestine.

Jesus is above the Holy Place, the temple. The charge against Stephen is that he has said Jesus will destroy the temple. (Acts 6:14; compare Mark 14:58; John 2:19.) Stephen's attack on the temple (Acts 7:44-50) is not simply the prophetic reminder that the spiritual transcends the material. He is thinking of the "Son of man" whose domain is universal. The "glory" that appeared to Abraham in Mesopotamia (Acts 7:2), that tabernacled with men in the tent all through the wilderness (Acts 7:44), that could never be confined to a temple made with hands (Acts 7:48), now appears fully revealed to Stephen in his vision of the heavenly "Son of man" (Acts 7:56). In this sense temple and law are indeed destroyed by Jesus. (Acts 6:11,13,14.) For with Him the prophecy has been fulfilled:

> . . . and the last (temple) shall be more glorious than the first. And the twelve tribes shall be gathered there, and all the Gentiles, until the Most High shall send forth His salvation in the visitation of an only-begotten prophet.[4]

With the coming of that One no temple was needed.

With Stephen's preaching of Jesus as the "Son of man" whose dominion transcends Jewish law, temple, race, and nation, the idea of the nature of Christ has reached a new stage. The Christian world mission begins.

Jesus as the Fulfiller of the Old Testament

Stephen echoed Peter's concept of Jesus as the Heavenly Deliverer and lifted that idea to new heights. He also developed the thought in Peter's sermons of Jesus as the Fulfillment of the Old Testament hope.

For Stephen, Jesus is not so much the fulfillment of this or that individual prophecy in Jewish Scripture; He is rather the fulfillment of the whole Jewish hope. All the process of Jewish history is seen as a frustration of hope until the goal is realized in Jesus. The Epistle to the Hebrews echoes this idea. What temple, king, and law could not do, Jesus has done.

A new element in Stephen's thought is his use of types and allegories to interpret the Old Testament as a witness to Christ. When this is understood the long, apparently rambling survey of Hebrew history becomes clearly meaningful.

Acts makes it clear that Stephen was a Hellenist, a Jew by race but bearing a Greek name and reared in a foreign culture. (Acts 6:1,5,9.) A peculiar allegorical method of interpreting Scripture developed among such men, as we know from the writings of Philo of Alexandria and others. Numerous similarities between Stephen's address and Philo's writings suggest that Stephen may have been influenced by these Hellenists. For example, both Philo and Stephen place Abraham in Mesopotamia, not Haran, for his call. Terah's death is said to have occurred before Abraham left Haran. The period of bondage is given as 400, not 430, years. The number of those who went down to Egypt is given as 75. The education and beauty of Moses are described. It is the desire to deliver Israel which prompts Moses' murder of the Egyptian. Angels give the law. All of this information came to Stephen from some source other than the Old Testament. But Philo, the Jewish teacher of Alexandria, tells us these things too. In Philo, the interpretation of the Old Testament through types and allegories is highly developed.[5] Even Palestinian rabbis sometimes allegorized Scripture, and there are a few traces of this method in Paul. (Galatians 4:24.) Allegory, therefore, could be quite natural for Stephen.

Allegorical interpretation of Scripture is dangerous and has often led to absurd extremes. Our purpose here, however, is not to pass judgment upon this method but, believing that Stephen did use it, to see what he was saying in this way about Jesus.

At two points the use of allegorical parallels by Stephen is relatively clear. In Acts 7:37 he pictures Moses as pointing to Jesus. And the attack in Acts 7:51-52 suggests a parallel between the rejection of the prophets and the rejection of Jesus. If one assumes further use of types and figures, much of the rest of the address, which otherwise seems, as Calvin said, "absurd and inept," now appears full of witness to Jesus.

For example, the lengthy account of the life of Joseph makes sense if we understand it as foreshadowing Jesus. Joseph's brethren deliver him into Egypt. But God raises him up and exalts him. Now Joseph becomes a saviour. So Jesus was betrayed, but is now exalted to be Saviour.

To take a debatable example, why does Stephen so often record that a *second* experience has been necessary to bring salvation in the past? Joseph was at first rejected by his brethren, accepted only at a second meeting. Moses had to have a successor, Joshua. The tabernacle was replaced by the temple. David needed a successor, Solomon. Is it not possible that Stephen is seeing these events as types of Christ, whom he preaches as rejected at first but coming a second time in triumph?

The clearest typology is that of Moses as a type of Christ. (Acts 7:37.) Perhaps the account of Moses' childhood (Acts 7:20-21) reflects some infancy story of Jesus, such as that in Matthew 2:13-18. Moses is especially chosen by God. Him "God sent as both ruler and deliverer." (Acts 7:35.) He is judge, leader, and prophet. He gives "living oracles" and bestows salvation (deliverance), being "mighty in his words and deeds." In him, as in all the prophets, there is foreshadowed "the coming of the Righteous One." (Acts 7:52.)

If this portrait of Moses is also intended as a portrait of Jesus, then Stephen adds a new title for Jesus, opening up a new and very important idea in Christian understanding. Moses is called the *redeemer* or *deliverer*. (Acts 7:35.) It is he who ransomed his kinsmen from slavery. So, it is implied, Jesus paid the price to set us free from sin.

If this typological interpretation of this address is correct, Stephen, building directly upon the preaching of Peter, opened up not only the idea of the Christian world mission but also a new approach to Jewish Scripture. It was a dangerous approach, one which was to lead to the extreme allegorizing on the part of some of the early church fathers in succeeding centuries. Rightly used, however, it led to new and very valuable discoveries about Jesus. The Epistle to the Hebrews shows how Stephen's ideas might be developed by an inspired writer.

Jesus' Earthly Life and His Exaltation

Stephen, like Peter, witnesses to the earthly life and the death of Jesus.

Stephen's portrait of Moses as the redeemer whose mighty words and deeds brought salvation to Israel is, in certain respects, if typologically interpreted, a portrait of Jesus as a man on earth. Especially do the rejection of Moses, of Joseph, and of the prophets parallel the rejection and crucifixion of Jesus.

As in the sermons of Peter, Jesus is pictured as now exalted to the right hand of God. It is true that Stephen gives no direct account of the Resurrection, but there can be no doubt that this is implied throughout his address. The exaltation of Joseph is probably intended as a type of the exaltation of Jesus. It was Stephen's cry concerning the exaltation of Jesus which precipitated the final onslaught. "Behold," he exclaimed, "I see the heavens opened, and the Son of man standing at the right hand of God." (Acts 7:56.) It was this "blasphemous" description of Jesus which brought Stephen's death.

Jesus as a Living and Present Power

Finally, Stephen, like Peter, sees Jesus as a living and present Power.

Like Peter, Stephen associates Jesus with the Holy Spirit. Jewish rejection of Jesus is seen as resistance to that Spirit. (Acts 7:51.) The coming of Jesus accomplishes, for Stephen, that tabernacling of the God of Glory with men which was never quite accomplished in the Old Testament.

To Stephen, Jesus is One present in the hour of need. Some have suggested that there is significance in the fact that

Stephen sees Jesus as standing, not sitting, at the right hand of God. Jesus has risen to defend His martyr, or perhaps to receive him. His appearance at this crisis shows His concern for Stephen.

The prayer of Stephen is highly significant. The figure of Jesus has not merged with that of God. Yet Stephen's dying cry is surely prayer, offered as to God. If in his plea "Lord Jesus, receive my spirit!" (Acts 7:59) there is an allusion to Psalm 31:1-5, then we are faced with the possibility that Stephen, here in the very earliest days of the church, thought of Jesus in these amazing terms:

> In thee, O Lord, do I seek refuge;
> . . . .
> Be thou a rock of refuge for me,
> a strong fortress to save me!
> . . . .
> for thou art my refuge.
> Into thy hand I commit my spirit;
> thou hast redeemed me, O Lord,
> faithful God.

Of one point about Stephen's idea of Jesus there is no uncertainty at all. Jesus was clearly the Lord of life and death. His claim upon Stephen was absolute. For Jesus, Stephen gave his life.

Conclusions

The study of the address attributed to Stephen in Acts 7 indicates three things about what the first preachers said of Jesus:

1. Stephen's address preserves for us a very early and independent witness that the ideas about Jesus found in the sermons attributed to Peter really were current in the early

church. Though originally from a different source this ancient document parallels at every major point the concept of Jesus found in the other sermons in Acts.

2. Stephen's address, however, does indicate something of the path by which later New Testament ideas about Jesus were to be developed. New discoveries in the Jewish Scriptures, the influence of Greek culture, and the continued experience of its Lord by the church in conflict here begin to lead to new realizations.

3. Stephen helped men to realize one fact about Jesus as important for our own day as for his: "The Son of man" transcends any one nation or race or sect. The Jesus of Stephen can never be thought of as the private deity of white people, or Americans, or Presbyterians, or any other one group. The Christ of the first martyr—the word means "witness"—still commands a world mission across every iron curtain of nation or segregration of race.

CHAPTER 9

JESUS in the Preaching of Paul

THERE CAN BE NO DOUBT about which of the early preachers proved the most effective missionary. One preacher—the Apostle Paul—clearly had the greatest influence on the thought of the church.

The Sermons of Paul

Paul's letters reveal his matured understanding of Jesus. His earliest extant Epistle (thought by many to be 1 Thessalonians), however, comes from perhaps twenty years after Paul's conversion. In two ways we can get behind the thought of Paul the letter writer to that of Paul the young missionary preacher: through the references in his letters to the early preaching (the *kerygma*) and through the sermons attributed to Paul in Acts.

Here, in Paul's own words, is the gospel as he first heard and preached it:

> . . . the gospel of God which he promised beforehand through his prophets in the holy scriptures, the gospel concerning his Son, who was descended from David according to the flesh and designated Son of God in power according to the Spirit of holiness by his resurrection from the dead, Jesus Christ our Lord . . . (Romans 1:1-4.)

> For I delivered to you as of first importance what I also received, that Christ died for our sins in accordance with the scriptures, that he was buried, that he was raised on

> the third day in accordance with the scriptures, and that he appeared to Cephas, then to the twelve . . . Last of all, as to one untimely born, he appeared also to me. . . . Whether then it was I or they, so we preach. (1 Corinthians 15:3-11.)[1]

Precisely those five ideas about Jesus found in the sermons attributed to Peter appear in such passages as these, reflecting the early preaching of Paul. Jesus is (1) the Heavenly Deliverer, "the Christ"; (2) the One "promised beforehand" in the Scripture; (3) the One whose death for our sins is so important that the subject of the preaching can sometimes simply be identified with "the cross"; (4) the One "declared to be the Son . . . by his resurrection"; and (5) the One who has now appeared to Paul as a living "Power."

A second source of information about Paul's preaching is the report given in Acts by his companion, Luke.

Early in his account of Paul's first missionary journey Luke records a sermon said to be given by Paul in the synagogue at Antioch in Pisidia. (Acts 13:16-41.) Luke appears to be presenting it as typical of the first preaching and especially of Paul's preaching. There are hints, however, that it may go back to the particular occasion of Paul's visit to Antioch.[2]

Its synagogue setting makes this sermon especially interesting. Paul begins in the typical manner of a synagogue "word of exhortation." (Acts 13:15-16.) How many of the first Christian sermons must have begun in the same way! The typical review of Scriptural history (Stephen began with a similar review but with a different emphasis in preaching to the synagogue of the Freedmen) may spring from two readings prescribed in the Jewish lectionary for a particular Sabbath. (Isaiah 1 and Deuteronomy 1.)[3]

As Foakes-Jackson comments on Acts 13:

> At whatever date Acts was written, the book gives an astonishingly convincing picture of the gospel as Paul presented it in his earliest recorded utterance.[4]

What can we learn from this sermon about the first ideas concerning Jesus?

Parallels Between the Sermons of Peter and Acts 13

Though different in form, setting, and origin, the sermon of Paul in Acts 13 closely parallels in content the sermons attributed to Peter. Precisely the same five ideas which Peter preached about Jesus reappear in the sermon of Paul.

The concept of Jesus as the Messiah of Jewish expectation, the Heavenly Judge, does not appear quite so clearly, though the sermon ends with the threat of judgment. (Acts 13:40-41. Acts 17:31, however, pictures Paul at Athens as warning that God "will judge the world in righteousness by a man whom he has appointed . . . ") Perhaps Paul's concept of Jesus as the One through whom the believer is justified, clearly reflected in Acts 13:38-39, produces this change of emphasis.

No sermon is more insistent upon the thought of Jesus as the Fulfillment of Scripture. Those who crucified Jesus did so out of ignorance of the Scripture, yet they were thereby fulfilling Scripture. (Acts 13:27,29.) The Resurrection, like the cross, was the fulfillment of prophecy. (Acts 13:32-34.) The coming judgment is that foretold in the Old Testament. (Acts 13:40-41.) The sending of Jesus is presented as the climax of God's redeeming action in history. The accent in Paul's account of Hebrew history is on a series of verbs. God *chose* Israel, *exalted* the people, *led* them *forth, carried* them *as a nursing father, destroyed* nations before them, *gave* them a land, *gave* them judges, and *raised up* David as king. The climax of his account of the Old Testament is the news that God has now raised up a Saviour, Jesus.[5] He is the ultimate embodiment of God's saving action in history.

Paul's account of Jesus as a man on earth closely parallels Peter's. Both begin with John the Baptist. (Acts 13:25; 10:37.) Both pass quickly over His sinless life to describe His prophesied death. (Acts 13:27-29; 10:39.)

The Resurrection is described with reference to the same Scriptural quotation, Psalm 16:10. (Acts 13:35; 2:31.)

Jesus is for both Peter and Paul the living and present Power, the Saviour (Acts 13:23; 5:31) who bestows forgiveness (Acts 13:38; 2:38). There is a strong hint in Paul's sermon of his development of this idea into the doctrine of "justification by faith." (Acts 13:39.)

Paul's sermon, then, is an additional witness that these were the first essential ideas about Jesus.

Jesus as the "Son of God"

One highly important idea about Jesus not mentioned by Peter or Stephen does appear in the sermon of Paul. For the first time in the sermons Jesus is called the Son of God.[6] (Acts 13:33.)

As originally used of Jesus, according to this passage at least, the concept of Jesus as the Son of God has explicit connection neither with the virgin birth on one hand nor with pagan myths about sons of gods on the other. Rather it is based on two Old Testament ideas.

First, Jesus is the Son of God in that He is the promised Messiah, the kingly Son of David. This is almost certainly the meaning of Acts 13:23, reflecting the prophecy:

> . . . I will establish the throne of his kingdom for ever. I will be his father, and he shall be my son. (2 Samuel 7:13-14.)

God's lovingkindness, the steadfast covenant love, will not depart from this Son of David. And thus the "Messianic" Second Psalm is quoted:

> Thou art my Son,
> today I have begotten thee.
> (Acts 13:33; compare Psalm 2:7.)

This Psalm lays emphasis on the universality of the dominion of the king: the nations become his inheritance. Originally this Psalm may have been sung at the coronation of a king. What the Old Testament kings never became, now Jesus is.

Paul presents David as uniquely the prototype of Christ. David is associated with the covenant promise, is raised up by God, and is acclaimed by God as a man after God's own heart. Jesus is now the promised Messiah of David's line. It is in this sense that He is the promised "Son of God."

But there is a second and deeper meaning to this idea that Jesus is God's Son. It is that Jesus is the One especially beloved by God and especially faithful to Him. The loving care of the Father is a recurring theme of this sermon. God chose "our fathers," Paul begins. God carried them as a nursing father in the wilderness. (Acts 13:18.) Saul and David are "sons." The promise made to the "fathers" concerning David's Son has now been fulfilled to the "children." (Acts 13:32-33.) It has been suggested that Deuteronomy 1 and Isaiah 1 form the background of the sermon.[7] Deuteronomy 1 tells how the fathers were rejected but the children were allowed to enter the promised land. The first chapter of Isaiah begins with the divine lament, "I have nourished and brought up children." The climax of Paul's sermon comes in the good news of God's true Son. Now the Father-Son relationship is at last established.[8] Jesus is the faithful and beloved Son of the Father. Though Israel was disobedient, Jesus has fulfilled all filial duty. He is indeed the "Son of God."

The Sermon at Athens

The sermon in Acts 17:22-31, Paul's address to the Greeks at Athens, brings us to the threshold of a completely new stage in the development of Christian thought. Now Paul is preaching to pagans, and he must proclaim Christ against a background not of Jewish Scripture but of Greek philosophy and culture. It is not Hebrew prophets that Paul quotes but teachers of Greece. (Acts 17:28.)

It is true that when in this sermon Paul turns to speak of Jesus the picture is essentially the same as in all the other sermons. Acts 17 presents no real blending of Greek and Hebrew thought. It simply hints at the beginning of that process. But in the days that followed, the church more and more began to proclaim Jesus not in Aramaic (first-century Hebrew) but in Greek, not in terms of the Jewish Scriptures alone but in terms of the world culture of the Greeks.

Conclusions

The study of the sermons of Paul leads to three conclusions:

1. Paul's sermons give additional support for the conclusions reached thus far. Peter's preaching, Stephen's preaching, the *kerygma* described in Paul's Epistles, and the sermons attributed to Paul in Acts—all contain the same

basic ideas about Jesus. The five concepts we have outlined really are what the first preachers said of their Master.

2. One important idea appears first in Acts in Paul's sermon in the Antioch synagogue: Jesus is the Son of God. This concept is derived from the Old Testament.

3. Paul's sermon at Athens indicates something of how thought about Jesus was to develop in the coming years as the gospel was presented in Greek terms. It was a marriage of Greek and Hebrew thought which gave birth to the New Testament writings and the great creeds of the church.

We shall see next how the earliest ideas about Jesus were developed and expanded, and yet preserved, by the New Testament writers as the Holy Spirit led them into new truth.

CHAPTER 10

JESUS in the New Testament Writings

The twenty-seven books of the New Testament describe Jesus in twenty-seven different ways. Yet all are based on the concept of Jesus which we have found in the first preaching.

To outline the various New Testament doctrines of the Person of Christ lies beyond the scope of this book. The purpose of this chapter is to show how these ideas developed from the first preaching about Jesus.

The books of the New Testament may be compared to the spokes of a wheel. Their ideas of Christ radiate from a common center: what the first preachers said about Jesus. Each writer tends to develop one or more of these fundamental ideas about Jesus. Some seek to relate two or more apparently conflicting ideas in the first witness to Christ. New environment and new experience bring progress in understanding. But in whatever direction his thought goes there is a sense in which each writer has as his starting point the "Christology" (the doctrine of the Person of Christ) found in the first preaching.

Revelation and the Heavenly Judge

For example, the book of Revelation develops the idea of Jesus as the Messiah of Jewish expectation, the Heavenly Deliverer, the Cosmic Judge. This idea has been found to be basic to the preaching of Peter.

Here is how the author of the Revelation pictured Jesus:

> Then I saw heaven opened, and behold, a white horse! He who sat upon it is called Faithful and True, and in righteousness he judges and makes war. His eyes are like a flame of fire, and on his head are many diadems; and he has a name inscribed which no one knows but himself. He is clad in a robe dipped in blood, and the name by which he is called is The Word of God. . . . From his mouth issues a sharp sword with which to smite the nations, and he will rule them with a rod of iron; he will tread the wine press of the fury of the wrath of God the Almighty. On his robe and on his thigh he has a name inscribed, King of kings and Lord of lords. (Revelation 19:11-16.)

Whence came this picture of Jesus as a gory Conqueror visiting the earth with heavenly judgment? And how can it find a place in the same New Testament with such different pictures of Jesus as the Friend of little children and the Great High Priest?

The answer lies in the earliest preaching about Jesus.

In the very beginning Peter interpreted the meaning of Jesus to his Jewish hearers in terms of the popular Jewish expectation of the day—transformed in many ways. Such weird books as Enoch had inspired in Jewish hearts the hope of a Cosmic Judge and Deliverer. That Jesus was the Fulfiller of this hope was a part of the first preaching.

The Revelation presents one expansion of this great idea. From that complex of ideas which described the Christ of the earliest Christians the writer of the Revelation seized upon this one above all the others to develop and extend. Here is one great spoke radiating from the center in the first preaching.

Every idea in the sermons of Peter that related Jesus to the Heavenly Judge is reflected in the Revelation.

The title "Christ," which by now has become almost just

another proper name to many New Testament writers, twice appears in the Revelation (11:15; 12:10) as a title bestowed upon Jesus as a Heavenly Being.

Jesus is now in heaven at the right hand of God (Revelation 5:6-7; compare Acts 2:33; 3:21), concealed till the Final Event. But it is the revelation of this concealed Figure which is the subject of the book of Revelation.

He brings the restoration of all things. (Revelation 21:5-6; compare Acts 3:21.)

And He brings the terrible judgment. (Revelation 19:11; compare Acts 10:42.)

He offers salvation through the conquest of God's enemies. (Revelation 19:1ff.; compare Acts 4:12.)

And He is uniquely related to that Spirit poured out at Pentecost and promised for the last days. (Revelation 1:10; 2:7, 11, 17, etc.; compare Acts 2:17.)

How the Revelation develops all these ideas is the subject for another book. Here we simply want to note that the Revelation is developing fully and completely one idea about Jesus found in the earliest preaching. This is the idea which the writer felt to be most meaningful for the church as it witnessed in the hostile pagan world. Jesus must be set in relation to the Roman Empire and the wholesale persecution by that empire of the early Christian witnesses. As this book was written men were being imprisoned, even killed, by the Roman authorities for the "crime" of being Christians. With inspired vision the author of the Revelation finds his hope in this great idea about Jesus: that however strong Rome may appear now, behind the scenes in heaven stands Christ, far mightier than the emperor, soon to conquer and to judge and even now revealed to the eyes of faith as holding His church in the palm of His hand!

Of course the Revelation does not omit entirely the other

ideas about Jesus found in the first preaching; each of them finds some place. But one concept is dominant: Jesus is the Heavenly Deliverer, the Cosmic Judge.

Hebrews and the Fulfiller of the Old Testament

The Epistle to the Hebrews emphasizes and develops in new ways the idea of Jesus as the Fulfiller of the Old Testament.

Here is how the author of Hebrews describes Jesus:

> . . . he holds his priesthood permanently, because he continues for ever. Consequently he is able for all time to save those who draw near to God through him, since he always lives to make intercession for them. For it was fitting that we should have such a high priest, holy, blameless, unstained, separated from sinners, exalted above the heavens. . . . who is seated at the right hand of the throne of the Majesty in heaven, a minister in the sanctuary and the true tent. (Hebrews 7:24–8:2.)

How different from the Revelation! How different it seems from the first preaching!

How did the Holy Spirit lead men to such ideas about Jesus? The answer is clear: by leading men to develop new implications in one of the great ideas of the first preaching about Jesus, that He is the Fulfiller of the Old Testament hope.

Every book of the New Testament develops this idea. Matthew, for example, must set Jesus' earthly life in relation to Old Testament prophecy. Romans works out the relationship between Jesus and the Old Testament law. But with unique emphasis Hebrews sets forth Jesus in Old Testament terms, and above these terms.

The thirteen chapters of Hebrews contain no less than

twenty-six extended quotations from the Jewish Scriptures! More than this, the whole purpose of the book is to set forth Jesus' relationship to all past revelation: Abraham, Moses, the prophets, the tabernacle, the priesthood, the angels, the law, the covenant, and especially God Himself. The Old Testament pictures of all of these, the author tells us, point to Jesus as the Fulfiller and Fulfillment, who transcends all previous revelation.

Peter, as we have seen earlier, applied to Jesus the Old Testament titles of the kingly Messiah, such as "Christ," "Son of David," and "Lord." These ideas now belong to those "elementary doctrines" (Hebrews 6:1) accepted by all Christains. The originally "Messianic" title which is of vital interest to the author of Hebrews is "the Son of God."

As used in the sermon in Acts 13, "Son of God" was derived from the Second Psalm, a song in praise of a king. Hebrews quotes the same Psalm, but the concept has now acquired much richer meaning. As *Son,* Jesus is above all prophets, priests, and even angels. Not simply in filial love but in nature He is related to God Himself.

Peter and Stephen described Jesus in terms of a Second Moses, a New Joshua, the *Pioneer* or *Captain*. Though this peculiarly Jewish concept seems to have been more or less abandoned by other New Testament writers it reappears in Hebrews. (2:10-18.) Here, however, it is lifted to new heights. Jesus has become a man, it is said, for the purpose of defeating the devil, destroying death, and setting the church free. The thought of Jesus as the *Pioneer* is now bound up with that of Jesus as the incarnate *Son* and the *Great High Priest.*

The thought of Jesus as the Great High Priest is the most distinctive idea of Hebrews; but it, too, is based on the first preaching. Peter, Stephen, and Paul saw Jesus foreshadowed in many and varied parts of the Old Testament. Now the author of Hebrews can see the whole catalogue of Scriptural heroes (Hebrews 11) pointing to Christ. The law (10:1) is but the shadow of the reality He has brought. With Him the sacrificial system ends, for He is the perfect and heavenly oblation. (Hebrews 7:27.) And thus Jesus can be described as the Great High Priest. What all the Old Testament priesthood foreshadowed, Jesus now is. In Him priest and sacrifice have become one. Yet this concept of Jesus as High Priest—in its way the very height of the New Testament teaching about Jesus and deserving many books itself—is based directly on a passage of Scripture cited by Peter in the sermon at Pentecost. (Psalm 110; Acts 2:34; Hebrews 5:6.)

Hebrews emphasizes the relationship of Jesus to the Old Testament, but it does not ignore the other ideas of the first preaching. For example, the author knows not only that Jesus is the Fulfillment of the Old Testament hope but that as the Heavenly Deliverer He transcends that hope. He works out the relationship between these two different ideas by reference to the Greek philosophical idea that there are two worlds: the real world, ideal and heavenly, and the apparent world, present and material. Tabernacle, law, and priesthood were but the earthly shadows of the transcendent, heavenly Reality. But in Christ that Reality has entered the material world. Thus all the Old Testament points to Jesus, but as the Cosmic Deliverer He transcends all.

The Synoptic Gospels and Jesus as a Man on Earth

The "synoptic" Gospels (Matthew, Mark, and Luke) expand the picture of Jesus as a man on earth. The Gospel writers clearly witness to their faith in the other major ideas about Jesus found in the first preaching. Mark (the earliest

Gospel) and the others are written to show that Jesus is the "Son of God." (Mark 1:1.) But their method of witness is to tell events of Jesus' earthly life.

Here is how Mark describes Jesus:

> And they were bringing children to him, that he might touch them; and the disciples rebuked them. But when Jesus saw it he was indignant, and said to them, "Let the children come to me, do not hinder them; for to such belongs the kingdom of God. Truly, I say to you, whoever does not receive the kingdom of God like a child shall not enter it." And he took them in his arms and blessed them, laying his hands upon them. (Mark 10:13-16; compare Matthew 19:13-15; Luke 18:15-17.)

Again one marvels at the contrast! The Heavenly Warrior of the Revelation, the Great High Priest of Hebrews, is also the human Friend of little children in the Gospels.

What unites these strangely different ideas is their common origin in the first preaching about Jesus. How closely the Gospels are related to the first preaching has been demonstrated by the British scholar C. H. Dodd in his book *The Apostolic Preaching and Its Developments*. Scholars called "Form Critics" have shown how the various stories of the Gospels give evidence of originating as illustrations in sermons.[1]

The preaching began its account of Jesus' earthly life with the story of His baptism by John. (Acts 10:37; 13:24.) Mark begins here also, and after a brief account of Jesus' birth Matthew and Luke take up their story here. For Mark, in the same sense as for Peter, Jesus' baptism is the "birth hour" of the Messiah. It is here that He is anointed by God with the Holy Spirit.

In the first sermons Jesus was called "the Prophet." Now

His prophetic teaching is recounted. The Form Critics have shown how many of the sayings of Jesus are told in the form of "pronouncement stories," short stories containing some saying of Jesus much in the form of illustrations from the early preaching. But Jesus is presented as clearly more than a prophet. Matthew pictures Him as giving the new law of God, a law transcending that of Moses.

Many of the stories of Jesus' deeds, His mighty works, reflect their origin as sermon illustrations. More detail is given the stories, but the purpose is the same. The stories of events in Jesus' life are told us not primarily to give us a systematic biography recounting the facts of Jesus' life but to show Jesus' authority, His power as the Son of God. At the same time they give a portrait of His sinless character as the perfect man.

Finally, just as the great event of Jesus' earthly life for the first preachers was His death, so the Gospels concentrate on the story of the cross. Nearly half of Mark is the account of the last week of Jesus' life, and Matthew and Luke also give this week a detailed report. Form Critics agree that this story is the oldest connected narrative portion of these writings. Here only can we trace, day by day, connected events in Jesus' life. Around this central fact of the preaching, detailed stories have clustered. Around the preaching of Jesus as the Crucified One, the Gospels were formed.

Paul and the Exalted One

The massive writings of Paul develop every idea of the first thoughts about Jesus. One idea especially developed in these letters is Peter's concept of Jesus as the Risen and Exalted One.

Here is how the Apostle Paul wrote of Jesus:

> He is the image of the invisible God, the first-born of all creation; for in him all things were created, in heaven and on earth, visible and invisible . . . through him and for him. He is before all things, and in him all things hold together. He is the head of the body, the church; he is the beginning, the first-born from the dead, that in everything he might be preëminent. For in him all the fullness of God was pleased to dwell. (Colossians 1:15-19.)

"The image of the invisible God . . . For in him all the fullness of God was pleased to dwell." What an exalted picture! What a contrast to the gory Warrior of the Revelation or the Friend of children in Mark! Yet Paul makes clear the basis for these "new" concepts: "the gospel which you heard, which has been *preached* . . . of which I, Paul, became a minister." (Colossians 1:23.)

Every idea of the first Jerusalem preaching about the Resurrection and exaltation is expanded by Paul. The Resurrection continues to be for him the heart of the Good News. "If Christ has not been raised, then our preaching is in vain and your faith is in vain." (1 Corinthians 15:14.) The Resurrection is the proof and the means of the exaltation. "Therefore God has highly exalted him and bestowed on him the name which is above every name, that at the name of Jesus every knee should bow." (Philippians 2:9-10.) It is a historical event. "Then he appeared to more than five hundred brethren at one time, most of whom are still alive." (1 Corinthians 15:6.) In the Resurrection, God vindicated the earthly life of His Son by divine action, and proclaimed His present status as the Christ. He was "designated Son of God in power . . . by his resurrection." (Romans 1:4.) And this is the guarantee of the final hope. "For since we believe that Jesus died and rose again, even so, through Jesus, God will bring with him those who have fallen asleep." (1 Thessalonians 4:14.)

This, then, was Paul's starting point: Jesus as the risen and exalted Christ. Indeed, it was his own personal experience of the Risen One that made Paul an apostle. (Galatians 1:15-17; 1 Corinthians 15:8-9; Ephesians 3:3.) How Paul built upon these original ideas is again the subject for another book. We shall examine briefly three ways in which the preaching of the Resurrection led Paul to the high concepts of Christ found in his Epistles.

First, Paul works out a relationship between Jesus as the Risen One and Jesus as the final Heavenly Deliverer. Jesus' resurrection is the guarantee of this future deliverance. He is "the first fruits of those who have fallen asleep." (1 Corinthians 15:20.) Thus, "since we believe that Jesus died and rose again, even so, through Jesus, God will bring with him those who have fallen asleep." (1 Thessalonians 4:14.) Because of the Resurrection, Christians await the "Son from heaven." (1 Thessalonians 1:10.)

Second, Paul's idea of the Risen Christ enables him to come to a new understanding of the relationship between Jesus and the Old Testament, especially the Old Testament law. By His resurrection, Jesus has conquered Satan and sin; and "the power of sin is the law." (1 Corinthians 15:56.) But those who are "in Christ" have died to sin and the law and have risen in Him to a new life of liberty. (Romans 6; Colossians 2:12-14.) Thus, it is by His resurrection that Jesus sets men free from the law.

Third, Paul as the great apostle to the Gentiles must deal with problems of a new and different kind. He must preach in Greek to Greeks, using the language of pagan philosophy, culture, and religion to express the original gospel. Colossians, for example, deals with questions of this newer kind which must be answered in terms of Greek thought. But again in presenting Jesus as "the image of the invisible God" (Colossians 1:15), in whom "the whole fulness of deity dwells bodily" (Colossians 2:9), Paul is careful to relate all that he is saying to the first preaching of the Resurrection. A pagan philosophy called "Gnosticism" or the competition of the heathen "mystery religions" of the time might drive Paul to new phrases and to new ideas, but for him it is the resurrection of Jesus which reveals all mysteries.

John and the Living and Present Power

The Gospel According to John illustrates the development of the idea of Jesus as a living and present Power.

Here is how John pictures Jesus:

> I am the bread of life. (John 6:35.)
> I am the light of the world. (8:12.)
> I am the good shepherd. (10:11.)
> I am the resurrection and the life. (11:25.)
> I am the vine, you are the branches. He who abides in me, and I in him, he it is that bears much fruit, for apart from me you can do nothing. (15:5.)

What a strange collection of books the New Testament is! Here in the same volume which has described Jesus as the Heavenly Conqueror on the white horse, the Great High Priest in the true tent, the Friend of little children, and the First-born from the dead—in this same book comes this picture of the Christ in the hearts of believers. He is called the Bread of Life, the Light of the World, the One in whom the Christian continually abides and whose Spirit dwells continually in us.

Yet once again the source of these ideas may be found in the first preaching.

We have seen how the first preachers pictured Jesus as

present Saviour and Lord of the fellowship of those who have been united to Him in faith and baptism, who gave to the fellowship power in His name, through the Spirit which He was pouring out upon them.

In the Fourth Gospel, Jesus is the One who baptizes with the Spirit still (1:33), His own ministry beginning when the Spirit descends upon Him. The new birth which He gives believers is of the Spirit. (3:5-8.) His words *are* "spirit." (6:63.) He offers to all the water of life through the outpouring of the Spirit. (7:38-39.) The great promise for the future in John is that the Spirit will come. (14:16-17; 15:26; 16:13.) The climax of the Gospel comes when Jesus breathes into the disciples His Spirit, forever empowering them. (20:22.)

But John's teaching about the Spirit goes beyond what this brief list of references might suggest. His whole account of Jesus' earthly life is designed to emphasize the abiding presence of Jesus with the believer here and now. For John, Jesus is the Saviour not so much in terms of some future judgment—for in Him judgment has already come (9:39; 12:31)—as in that He brings rebirth (3:3), living water (7:38), new and abundant life (10:10), in the present for all eternity.

Thus the concept of Jesus' present Lordship over the church, the seeds of which are in Acts, develops into a faith in full mystical union between the believer and his Lord. Christ is now related to the community by a continual abiding, He in them and they in Him. (John 15:4.) Obedience, love, and faith bring a mystical relationship only hinted at in the first preaching.

Not only does John carry to new heights the idea of Jesus as a living and present Power found in the first preaching; he also makes two other special contributions to the doctrine of the nature of Christ.

First, John strives to reconcile two seemingly contradictory ideas in the first preaching about Jesus. Is Jesus a living and present Power? Or is He the still-hoped-for coming Cosmic Judge? John's answer is that future hope is already being fulfilled for the believer in the abiding presence of Christ. John does not completely abandon future expectation (John 5:28-29; 14:3), but the "second coming" which he emphasizes is the coming of the Holy Spirit. The first three Gospels record a discourse on the final judgment just before the story of Jesus' death. (Matthew 24; Mark 13; Luke 21.) John records instead the promise of the coming of the Comforter, the Spirit. (John 14:26; 15:26; 16:13.) Jesus is the One who sends this Spirit. Thus, even though the world does not see Him, the disciples know that He has already come. (John 14:19.) Standing on this side of the Resurrection, John can see the events of the earthly life of Jesus in a new and continuing glory. The "first coming" has already brought the judgment (John 9:39; 12:31), the resurrection (John 11:25), the eternal life (John 5:24; 6:63) for those who have faith to see it. In Him the glories of the Messianic Age are already being realized. He *is* the Resurrection and the Life.

The second special factor in the thought of John about Jesus is his relating Christ to the "Word." (John 1:1-14.) John here remains true to his heritage in Jewish thought. (Proverbs 8 speaks of the pre-existent *word,* or *wisdom* of God.) But the "Word" (Greek, *logos*) was also a Greek philosophical concept which would have meaning to the Roman world. Here, as elsewhere in the New Testament, one sees the influence of Greek language and ideas. Translation of the good news into the Greek language and the expression of the meaning of Jesus in terms of Greek ideas was part of the process that, beginning with Peter's preaching, produced the great Christian creeds.

Conclusions

"What do you think of the Christ?" We have now asked this question of the New Testament writers and have gotten an amazing variety of answers. "He is a blood-stained Warrior," says the Revelation. "He is the Priest in the Heavenly Tabernacle," says Hebrews. "He is One who took children in His arms," say the Gospels. "He is the First-born from the dead," says Paul. "He is the Bread of Life," says John.

Yet for each of these divergent ideas we have found a common basis. It is the first preaching about Jesus, the kind of preaching recorded for us with what now appears to be remarkable accuracy in the book of Acts.

We have examined in detail these first sermons, learning from them the very first ideas about Jesus preached in the primitive Jerusalem church. In this chapter we have studied what happened to these ideas, how the New Testament writers developed their thoughts about Him. A threefold process has been discovered:

1. Particular ideas of the first preaching about Jesus were extended and developed. The various New Testament concepts of Jesus radiate, each in its own direction, from a center found in the preaching, like spokes from the hub of a wheel. The author of the Revelation develops the idea of Jesus as the Coming Judge. Mark develops the first accounts of Jesus as a man on earth. John expands the thought of Jesus as a living and present Power. This is not to say that each writer abandons all other concepts. (For example, Mark is writing to show that Jesus is the Son of God.) But it is the particular task of each of the various writers to develop one of the concepts of the early preaching.

2. New Testament writers seek to establish the relationship between diverse and sometimes seemingly conflicting

ideas about Jesus found in the first preaching. For example, John harmonizes the thought of Jesus as the Messiah of the Last Days with that of His continuing presence and of His earthly life. Paul relates the Crucified and Risen One to the Old Testament law. The author of Hebrews works out his own synthesis of the transcendence of the Final Judge and the Christ of the Old Testament hope.

3. Primitive Jewish thought about Jesus now comes into contact with Greek ideas, and the church finds itself in the midst of new experiences. Many of these ideas and experiences the church finds it can use to advantage, at the same time expressing itself through and enriching itself by means of Greek thought. In this transition we enter the third great stage in the development of the doctrine of the person and nature of Christ, the working out of the early Christian creeds. In the first chapter of this book there is a quotation from the classic Nicene Creed, a product of the fourth century. How different it is from the sermon at Pentecost! And yet, point by point, how closely it is related to the first preaching!

Perhaps the classic creeds only made explicit what was implicit in the earliest ideas about Jesus. He is indeed "very God and very man."

CHAPTER 11

What Do You Think of THE CHRIST?

"WHAT DO YOU THINK OF THE CHRIST? Whose Son is he?"

The purpose of this book has been to find the very earliest answers to this question. We have sought to go behind the first creeds of the church. We have even endeavored to go behind the books of the New Testament themselves. We have attempted a great adventure, the exploration of that dark tunnel between the known historical fact of the cross and the light of the earliest New Testament writings. Through scientific research we have asked our question of the witnesses closest to the Christ-event in history. We have tried as twentieth-century Christians to think again the thoughts of members of the Jerusalem church of A.D. 30.

To describe the Christ of the earliest Christians we have examined the first Christian sermons; we have studied the ideas about Jesus found in the preaching reported in that ancient and fascinating document, the book of Acts.

The Reliability of Acts

To begin, it was necessary to examine this source with sceptical caution. It was found that as a historical source Acts measures up well. Acts, though written probably fifty years after the events it describes, comes from the pen of an early Christian missionary, a companion of the great preacher Paul. Luke is a demonstrably accurate historian. There are clear signs that in his early chapters he makes use of historically valuable sources. And parallel passages in the writings of Paul make clear that the sermons Luke records are indeed typical of the first Christian preaching.

Moreover, the ideas about Jesus presented in these sermons have been seen to fit best their Jerusalem setting, standing in contrast to later Greek ideas.

There is good reason, therefore, to believe that the sermons in Acts do give an accurate report of the answer of the first preachers to the question, "What do you think of the Christ?"

Some Popular Fallacies

The answer to our question has proved quite surprising. Many scholars and many popular theories about the beginnings of Christianity have been found to be in error.

For example, many a modern sceptic and many a "liberal" Christian has supposed that the church began with the thought of Jesus simply as a great and good man. It has been said that Christianity began as the memory of the "simple religion of Jesus," His teachings and His example. Paul and others "ruined" Christianity, runs the argument, by transforming it literally into a hero-worship that made Jesus into a kind of God.[1] A scientific study of the New Testament, thousands have been led to believe, shows the development from the simple idea of Jesus to the complex, from the "low" to the "high," from the idea of Jesus as a man to the idea of Jesus as God.

If our study has been correct, this theory is shattered. The truth is that it is impossible to penetrate back to a time in the history of the church when the Risen Christ was not looked upon as a Divine Being. Go back in the dark tunnel as far as anyone can, go all the way to the Day of Pentecost; there was no time when His disciples looked upon Jesus simply as their teacher. From the very beginning He was proclaimed to be the heavenly Son of man in utterly transcendent terms. From the beginning He was assigned attributes heretofore reserved strictly for God. This is not at all to say that Peter at Pentecost stated clearly, or understood clearly, that "Jesus is God." This is not to say that the church began by splitting hairs over the doctrine of the nature of Christ, as the church was to do 300 years later. It is to say, however, that when, at the climax of his Gospel, John pictured Thomas as calling Jesus "My Lord and my God" this was not an entirely new concept. The seeds had been sown in the first preaching.

But, surprisingly enough, we have also found to be wrong the view at the opposite extreme. Most modern Christians, reciting the creeds or studying the catechisms, probably suppose that these report the first ideas about Jesus. And would-be orthodox theologians have attempted to prove that all the ideas of the later creeds and catechisms were present in the church from the beginning. A Greek myth pictured Athena as being born full-grown. It was not so with the church's understanding of Christ. All the words of the Nicene Creed and the Westminster Standards may well be true, but it is highly doubtful that Peter could have said them at Pentecost. At least there is no indication that he actually did so. "Very God of very God . . . of one substance with the Father . . ." "in two distinct natures, and one person . . ." This is the language of centuries later. The earliest preaching was something different even from the New Testament teaching. The Spirit had to lead the church to new truth.

The views of many of the really great Biblical students of Europe concerning the first ideas about Jesus are also found to be inadequate. For example, certain professors of the "form-critical" school have argued that the first Christians had little interest in the earthly life of Jesus except to affirm His saving death. This preoccupation with the "spiritual" to the neglect of the "historical" Jesus cannot really be found in Acts. The emphasis was indeed on the cross. But the picture of Jesus' deeds, teachings, and character also had its place. Martin Dibelius is, in a sense, quite right that "there never was a 'purely' historical witness to Jesus." [2] All that was preached of His life was as a witness to the meaning of that life. But the first preaching did not neglect "the Jesus of history." On the other hand, scholars like Wilhelm Bousset and Albert Schweitzer have seen the first great idea about Jesus to be that of Christ as the heavenly Son of man, the Coming Judge. Our discovery is that this is too simple an answer. This apocalyptic idea had its place, but it was modified by many other ideas about Jesus, some quite contradictory, which are equally old. Another widely held view is that of Johannes Weiss, that the church first thought of Jesus as one born a man but later adopted to become the Son of God. The sermons in Acts do show a unique emphasis on the exaltation, the startling contrast between what Jesus was as God's Servant and what He became as the church's Lord. But the change which was said to have taken place was one of status, from "Servant" to "Lord," not of nature, from "man" to "God." Greek myths of adoption offer no genuine analogy to what is found in Acts.

What the First Preachers Said About Jesus

What the first preachers said about Jesus has been found to be no one of the above answers, but all of them. Each of these ideas has a place. The error of so many thinkers is that they have assumed too simple a starting point for the primitive idea of Jesus. Actually, what we have found is that the Christ of the earliest Christians was amazingly complex. The first preaching was filled with richly varied ideas about Jesus —often quite contradictory ideas—welded together not by logical system but by the ecstatic experiences of the time. As far back as research can take us we find the church witnessing to its Lord in terms derived partly from Jewish apocalyptic literature, partly from the Old Testament canon, partly from its clear memory of Jesus' earthly life, and partly from the experiences of the Resurrection and the repeated outpourings of the Holy Spirit.

Exploration must take the twentieth-century Christian back into the weird world of the first-century Jewish apocalyptic literature and popular hope. Men like Schweitzer and Bousset are right; the Christ of the earliest Christians was described in terms like that of the Son of man in the Book of Enoch. He was thought of as the angelic Judge of angels and devils, good men and bad, the living and the dead. He was called "the Righteous One," destined to conquer Satan and in awful triumph to save His elect. He was preached as an utterly supernatural Heavenly Being, the Spirit-filled Agent of God's judgment. His coming, it was said, had brought all of history to its climactic stage.

"What do you think of the Christ?" the modern Christian asks the first Christian preachers. Their second answer is this: "To him all the prophets bear witness." (Acts 10:43.)

To understand the Christ of the earliest Christians the twentieth-century student must go not only into the world of Jewish apocalyptic hope but also into the rich resources of the Old Testament canon. The Old Testament of the early church is a radically reinterpreted Scripture in which everything points to Jesus. He is described in terms of the transcendent King of the Old Testament promise, the Son of David who was at the same time David's Lord, the Christ who was the embodiment of all the hope of Hebrew history and yet much more, the One peculiarly related to the Hebrews' God and possessing divine authority. He was described as a kind of second Moses, a new and greater Joshua, founding and leading a new community of the redeemed, voicing a new and final revelation of God's will, embodying the culmination of the prophetic office. He was indeed the personal representative of all the Hebrew nation's history and mission and the Fulfiller and Fulfillment of all its previously unfulfilled hope and destiny. He was the truly Holy, the Anointed One of its priestly cult, at the same time Priest and Sacrifice. And He was repeatedly described in terms not simply of the Old Testament Messiah but of the Old Testament God. One is awed by the majesty of these thoughts.

"What do you think of the Christ?" one asks today. And the first preachers reply in terms which reflect a precious memory still fresh in their minds. The Christ of the earliest Christians is:

> Jesus of Nazareth, a man attested to you by God with mighty works and wonders and signs which God did through him in your midst, as you yourselves know. (Acts 2:22.)

Jesus is the Messiah, they said; but also the Messiah is Jesus! The first preachers were not primarily concerned to give new interpretations to Jewish Scriptures but to spread the good news about Him who "went about doing good." His human nature and origin were clearly affirmed. His baptism, His teachings, His "mighty works," and His moral character were described. And especially was His death seen to have saving meaning. He is called the "Servant," the One who gave His life as a ransom for many. The earliest preaching is the preaching of the cross.

"What do you think of the Christ?" Perhaps the answer of the earliest Christians which seems strangest to modern minds is that He is the One who was exalted.

> God has made him both Lord and Christ, this Jesus whom you crucified. (Acts 2:36.)

The Resurrection, with its complete surprise, was still fresh in the mind of the church, a material and spiritual fact. He who had died as Servant had been raised as Lord. The Resurrection did not mean simply the immortality of Jesus. It was at the same time the vindication of His earthly ministry and the proclamation of His divine status, His being at the right hand of God. The contrast between what Jesus had been and what He had become—not in nature, as in the Greek myths, but in status, from Servant to Lord—fills the first preachers with glad amazement.

> The Head that once was crowned with thorns
> Is crowned with glory now.[3]

Jesus, who died on the Roman cross, is raised to a new position, not clearly defined, distinct from and yet equal to God, at God's right hand.

"What do you think of the Christ?" The final answer which the first Christians would give to Christians of today is this: He is a living and present Power. The exhortation of the first preachers is:

> . . . be baptized every one of you in the name of Jesus Christ for the forgiveness of your sins; and you shall receive the gift of the Holy Spirit. (Acts 2:38.)

Not only in the past, future, and perfect tenses did the primitive church speak of its Lord, but also in the present tense.

Jesus was related, they were sure, in some way which they did not always define, to the Holy Spirit's repeatedly being poured out upon them in ecstasy and power. His name was sufficient to produce miracles of healing and exorcism. He was the present agent of the divine forgiveness and salvation. He was the Lord of the church, the object of its devotion, its personal and present Head. He was in deed if not in name really its God.

This was the beginning. We cannot discover a time when thought about Jesus was "lower" or simpler. This is the Christ of the earliest Christians.

The Development of These Ideas

The modern Christian can see how these ideas developed.

There is little in Acts to confirm Wernle's theory of a kind of development backward, in which Jesus is said to have been thought of as becoming divine first at His second coming, then at His resurrection, then at His baptism, then at His birth, and finally as being pre-existent. We can discover no steady progress from a "low" view of Jesus as a man to a "high" view of Jesus as God. Certainly there is no clearly expressed Trinitarian creed in the beginning. Nor is there progress from a simple idea of Jesus to a complex one.

Almost the reverse is the case. The original idea of Christ we have found to be surprisingly complex. The progress from it has been likened to the radiation of spokes from the center of a wheel. The New Testament writers each developed one or more of these basic ideas about Jesus found in the first preaching. The Heavenly Conqueror, the Great High Priest, the Friend of children, the First-born from the dead, the Vine—all the pictures of Jesus in the New Testament derive directly from these earliest ideas about Jesus.

Again, the New Testament writers endeavored to work out the relationship of the seemingly conflicting ideas about Jesus in the first preaching, how He who was the future Hope was also a present Reality.

Finally, the preaching of the gospel to a Greek world, the persecution by the Roman authorities, the competition of the pagan mystery religions, the rich ideas of Greek philosophy—all these forced the church to express its eternal message in new ways. The Spirit used the Gentile world to lead the church to new truth. Ultimately the great systematic doctrines about Jesus, "Christology," came into being in the form of carefully thought-out creeds. Pentecost had led to Nicea.

"What Do You Think of the Christ?"

"What do you think of the Christ?" Jesus Himself asks this question. The purpose of this book has been to describe the answer that comes from the days closest to His earthly life.

At first the answer that has been found may seem disappointing. The Christ of the earliest Christians may seem to the twentieth-century American a strange, exotic Person, completely removed from us by race, nation, and time. In a dead language, Aramaic, the first preachers described Jesus in terms of the curious Jewish expectation of a kind of superangel who would destroy demons at the end of the world. They strained for questionable meanings from their sacred books to describe Him. He appears in the first sermons as an obscure miracle worker in a backward country two thousand years ago. The concept of Jesus as the Exalted One is so strange that it is often forgotten today. And at first the westerner may feel quite uncomfortable with so Oriental an idea as that of Jesus as the Healing Name. One is tempted to cry with the demon-possessed man of old, "What have you to do with me, Jesus?" (Mark 5:7.)

Yet precisely because they did bear witness to Jesus in language and forms which had real meaning to human beings in an actual place at a definite time, the first preachers have shown us a significant Christ. Translated from the Aramaic language and transposed from Palestine and the past, their ideas are found to be packed with dynamic meaning for every age and land.

They called Jesus a Cosmic Judge who would conquer the world and deliver His people at the end of the age. Unfortunately, the idea of world conquest is not unknown in our own day. Many a twentieth-century Christian has found that his very life depended on his answer to the question, "Which conqueror do you choose? Jesus, or our dictator?" Joel's sign of the red moon in the heavens seems like a prophecy of our own headlines. We are aware that we, too, live at the end of an age. Granted that we must reinterpret the idea of the Jewish apocalyptic deliverer; the first Christians reinterpreted him, too. In the cosmic warfare we may well sing,

> For not with swords' loud clashing,
> Nor roll of stirring drums,
> With deeds of love and mercy,
> The heavenly kingdom comes.[4]

Yet in a day when psychologists are only beginning to discover what devils lurk in the dim recesses of our minds and when the skies are filled with ever more hellish weapons of destruction, Christians are grateful that Christ is the Heavenly Deliverer. There is salvation nowhere else.

The first Christians were so sure that Jesus was everywhere witnessed to in the Old Testament that it may seem to modern Christians that they twisted and distorted many of their texts. The stone which the builders rejected (Acts 4:11; Psalm 118:22) was, in the mind of the psalmist, the Hebrew nation. It is highly unlikely that the first hearers of Psalm 16 saw in its reference to flesh which would not see corruption a prophecy of the resurrection of Christ. (Acts 2:31.) Yet the very strainedness of their use of Scripture shows how convinced the first Christians were that Jesus was to be understood in the light of the whole Old Testament. If the modern Christian is to come to an understanding of the meaning of Jesus he must find that understanding, in large measure, as he studies the Old Testament. His study must not be confined to a few passages in which prophets speak of a promised Messiah. To understand Jesus fully we must understand all the Old Testament's revelation of the purpose of God, all the Old Testament's concept of the mission and destiny of the people of God—indeed, all the Old Testament's revelation of the character and will of God Himself. If anyone wants to know the meaning of Jesus he must search for that meaning in The Book.

Granted that the Christ of the earliest Christians was a man of an alien race and a foreign place, this is our guarantee that He was of the human race and an earthly place. Peter's Jesus is no dream, no myth, no angel. He is a flesh-and-blood man exactly as we are men—born, speaking, doing deeds, dying. He is a fact of history which no sceptic need doubt. Other religions may rest on legends which research may disprove. Christianity, however, is an interpretation of an irrefutable fact, the life and death of Jesus. New ages may produce new understanding of how the death of Jesus saves. But the first preachers began by pointing lost men to the cross.

The exaltation of Jesus was a theme of every sermon in

Acts. Churchgoers hear few sermons about it today. The idea that Jesus was made Christ at His exaltation has largely been replaced in the thought of most Christians by the realization that He was born Christ, even pre-existed as Christ. Yet for our day the unique emphasis of the first preaching on the exaltation is a clear witness that the resurrection of Jesus is true. The first preachers described the contrast between what Jesus had been and what He had now become with a note of surprise too joyful to be insincere. The first sermons help prove the Resurrection fact. They also remind us that the essential Easter message is not a general truth about immortality but good news about Jesus. The Resurrection stands as the great sign of things still true: His triumph and His continuing presence.

Finally, the Christian who has never spoken with tongues nor cast out demons through the Name may still meet the Christ of personal experience. The kind of experience of Jesus as a living and present Power which is characteristic of the twentieth century is not entirely identical with that of the first. But the Christ who pours out His Spirit upon the heart of the believer is the same in every age. New experience teaches new understanding. But still as of old men meet Jesus, alive and with them, working miracles in them and through them, saving them into the church of which He is the Personal Lord. And those who thus daily meet the Risen Christ may cry with Thomas, "My Lord and my God!"

A Postscript

It is not enough to know what the first preachers said about Jesus. Jesus' question, "What do you think of the Christ?" has meaning for men in every age. The New Testament writers were not content simply to parrot Peter's sermon at Pentecost. They described Jesus in the language and the thought forms of the people to whom they wrote, and against the background of new inspiration and experience. The church was not content simply to quote the New Testament, but proclaimed its faith in the carefully worded creeds of the fourth and fifth centuries. The Reformers, without disputing these creeds, preached Jesus in the light of new problems and new experience. It is the task of Christians in every age to find new meaning in Jesus. It is the promise of Christ that we are not without help in this task. (John 16:12-15.) Beginning then with what the first preachers said about Jesus, but relating Him to your citizenship in the modern world—your job, your home, your life—you find that still Jesus asks, "What do *you* think of the Christ?"

Notes and Acknowledgments

Chapter 1

The Christ of the Earliest Christians

1. From the Nicene Creed as found in *The Book of Common Worship,* inside back cover. Philadelphia: The Board of Christian Education of the Presbyterian Church in the United States of America, 1946.
2. Albert Schweitzer, *The Quest of the Historical Jesus,* translated by W. Montgomery. New York: The Macmillan Company, 1948.
3. The basic idea of even the earliest Gospel, Mark, is that Jesus is far more than just "a man among men." For Mark, He is "the Son of God." The Gospels, however, do present our most detailed portrait of the human Jesus. The emphasis developed is different from that of Paul's letters or of the Revelation.
4. "Under the influence of the Messianic dogmas, and led by the impression which Christ made, Paul became the author of the speculative idea that not only was God in Christ, but that Christ himself was possessed of a peculiar nature of a heavenly kind." Adolf Harnack, *What is Christianity?,* translated by Thomas Bailey Saunders, p. 199. New York: G. P. Putnam's Sons, 1901. Used by permission.
5. See Johannes Weiss, "Acts of the Apostles" in *A Dictionary of Christ and the Gospels,* p. 27, James Hastings, editor. New York: Charles Scribner's Sons, 1906. See also Johannes Weiss, *Christ, the Beginnings of Dogma,* translated by V. D. Davis, p. 43. London: Philip Green, 1911.
6. G. S. Duncan, *Jesus, Son of Man,* pp. 3,4. New York: The Macmillan Company, 1949. Used by permission.

Chapter 2

Acts and the Earliest Answer

1. "The Muratorian Canon," dating from around A.D. 200, states: "Moreover, the Acts of all the Apostles are included in one book. Luke addressed them

to the most excellent Theophilus, because the several events took place when he was present; and he makes this plain by the omission of the passion [death] of Peter and of the journey of Paul when he left Rome for Spain." Quoted in *Documents of the Christian Church,* p. 40, Henry Bettenson, editor. New York: Oxford University Press, 1947. Used by permission.

2. Colossians 4:14; 2 Timothy 4:11; Philemon 24; and possibly Romans 16:21.
3. For arguments against the Lukan authorship of Acts see Hans Windisch, "The Case Against the Tradition," in *The Beginnings of Christianity,* Vol. II, pp. 298-348, F. J. Foakes Jackson and Kirsopp Lake, editors. London: Macmillan and Co., Ltd., 1922. Windisch is effectively answered by Vincent Taylor in *The Expositor,* Series 9, Vol. IV, pp. 282-291. London: Hodder and Stoughton, Ltd., 1925. A more recent detailed discussion supporting the traditional view is that of G. H. C. Macgregor in *The Interpreter's Bible,* Vol. IX, pp. 19-21, George Buttrick, editor. Nashville: Abingdon-Cokesbury Press, 1954.
4. Sir William M. Ramsay, *The Bearing of Recent Discovery on the Trustworthiness of the New Testament,* pp. 35-64. London: Hodder and Stoughton, Ltd., 1915. Used by permission.
5. See, for example, G. H. C. Macgregor, *op. cit.,* p. 10.
6. For a list of these difficulties see Hans Windisch, *op. cit.,* pp. 298-348. See also John Knox, *Chapters in a Life of Paul,* chapters 1-5. Nashville: Abingdon-Cokesbury Press, 1950. Though in the body of our book we have presented only the evidence in favor of Luke's accuracy it must here be noted that there are real problems in this connection. The biggest difficulty is to reconcile Acts with Paul's own account of his life given in Galatians 1 and 2. For example, Paul tells in Galatians 2:1-10 of a conference in Jerusalem on the matter of circumcision. Acts 15 reports a conference on the same subject. The two accounts vary, however, in many important details. Acts indicates that the conference occurred on Paul's third visit to Jerusalem after his conversion. Galatians assures us that it was on his second visit. Some of this difficulty can be eliminated if one holds (with Macgregor, *op. cit.,* pp. 150-152,198, and others) that Galatians 2 refers to discussions which took place during Paul's second visit to Jerusalem (Acts 11:30), not to the Jerusalem assembly described in Acts 15. Other discrepancies may be explained by the fact that Paul here is writing in the heat of controversy to prove one point, while Acts is written years later for a very different purpose. Many questions about the relationship of Galatians to Acts will never be settled. For our purposes, however, it is not necessary to be certain that Luke's chronology is infallible or that he has always combined his sources smoothly. It is enough that we should see that he did have access to highly valuable sources of information. We shall still find it necessary to check the ideas found in the sermons he

records to see how well they fit historically into their early Jerusalem setting. This we will attempt to do as these ideas are described.

7. For a list of theories about the sources of the book of Acts see R. J. Knowling, "The Acts of the Apostles," in *The Expositor's Greek Testament,* Vol. II, pp. 16 ff., W. Robertson Nicoll, editor. Grand Rapids: William B. Eerdmans Co. (n.d.)
8. W. L. Knox, *St. Paul and the Church at Jerusalem,* page 90, footnote. Cambridge: The University Press, 1925. Used by permission.
9. See B. S. Easton, *Christ in the Gospels,* pp. 4-5. New York: Charles Scribner's Sons, 1928.
10. J. Klausner, *From Jesus to Paul,* p. 218. New York: The Macmillan Company, 1943. Used by permission.
11. Especially Charles C. Torrey, *The Composition and Date of Acts,* pp. 3-41. Cambridge: Harvard University Press, 1916. Many of the Greek phrases of the early chapters of Acts appear to him to suggest an Aramaic original. A large number of his best examples are taken from the sermons in Acts.
12. For example, J. deZwaan, in Jackson and Lake, *The Beginnings of Christianity,* Vol. II, pp. 30-65. More recently Matthew Black writes: "The most likely places where Semitic sources were used by Luke, apart from the sayings of Jesus, are in the first two chapters of his Gospel and in the speeches of Peter and Stephen in the early chapters of Acts." Matthew Black, *An Aramaic Approach to the Gospels and Acts,* p. 207. Oxford: The Clarendon Press, 1946. Used by permission.
13. Henry J. Cadbury demonstrates this and argues on this basis that the speeches in Acts are "devoid of historical basis in genuine tradition." Henry J. Cadbury, "The Speeches in Acts," in Jackson and Lake, *The Beginnings of Christianity,* Vol. V, pp. 402-427. London: Macmillan and Co., Ltd., 1933.
14. Thucydides, *Peloponnesian War,* Book I, Chapter 22, Jowett translation.
15. See Ernest F. Scott, *The Varieties of New Testament Religion,* p. 22. New York: Charles Scribner's Sons, 1943.
16. The Greek verb *euaggelizo,* "to preach the gospel," seems to be synonymous with *kerusso,* "to preach," in the New Testament.
17. These passages, according to Dodd, are 1 Corinthians 15:1-7; 1 Thessalonians 1:10; Romans 1:1-4; 2:16; 8:34; 10:8-9; and Galatians 1:3-4; 3:1; 4:6.
18. C. H. Dodd, *The Apostolic Preaching and Its Developments,* p. 17. New York: Harper & Brothers, 1936. Used by permission.

Chapter 3

Jesus, the Messiah of Jewish Expectation

1. All quotations from the Pseudepigrapha, except those from Enoch, are from *The Apocrypha and Pseudepigrapha of the Old Testament in English,* Vol. II, R. H. Charles, editor. Oxford: The Clarendon Press, 1913. Used by permission. Quotations from Enoch are from R. H. Charles, *The Book of Enoch.* Oxford: The Clarendon Press, 1893.
2. See the translations of "The Damascus Document" and "The Manual of Discipline" in Millar Burrows, *The Dead Sea Scrolls,* pp. 355,361,383. New York: The Viking Press, 1955. Used by permission.
3. The Book of Enoch, sometimes called I Enoch, was well known even before the discovery of the Dead Sea Scrolls, but largely through Ethiopic and Greek versions. The recent finding of so many Aramaic manuscripts makes clear its popularity, previously disputed, in first-century Palestine. The classic English translation is that of R. H. Charles. Charles dates the original work in the second century B.C. He feels that nearly every book of the New Testament reflects the influence of *The Book of Enoch.*
4. Daniel 9:25-26 does mention "an anointed one, a prince," but he is not a figure comparable to Peter's "Christ." He reigns for only sixty-two weeks, then is cut off, never to appear again. The use of the word in Daniel, however, does confirm its association with "apocalyptic" literature like Daniel, Enoch, and certain of the Dead Sea scriptures.
5. According to R. H. Charles, *The Book of Enoch,* p. 51.
6. See Jackson and Lake, *The Beginnings of Christianity,* Vol. IV, p. 83. London: Macmillan and Co., Ltd., 1933.
7. For example, in Justin Martyr, *Dialogue with Trypho,* Chapter 8, a Jew describes the hidden Messiah. Thomas B. Falls, *Writings of Saint Justin Martyr,* pp. 160-161, in the series, *The Fathers of the Church,* Ludwig Schopp, editor. New York: Christian Heritage, Inc., 1948.
8. See Acts 3:21. Some scholars, including the translators of the Revised Standard Version, translate the Greek word here simply as *establishing* in the sense of fulfillment of prophecy. The basic meaning of the word, however, is *restoration,* and in the context of "times of refreshing" (3:19) this "apocalyptic" meaning seems the correct one.
9. The one significant exception is the "apocalyptic" book, Daniel, where "Michael" may possibly be the judge meant. (Daniel 12:1-2.) Here is another hint of the ties between the first preaching and the "apocalyptic" literature.
10. Psalm 106:21; Isaiah 43:3; Jeremiah 14:8.
11. From "The Manual of Discipline" as translated by Millar Burrows, *The Dead Sea Scrolls,* pp. 375-376.

CHAPTER 4

JESUS, THE FULFILLER OF THE OLD TESTAMENT

1. The Dead Sea scrolls contain a collection of Old Testament quotations justifying the Messianic ideas of their community. See also Rendel Harris, *Testimonies,* Cambridge: The University Press, 1916. Also see B. P. W. Strather Hunt, *Primitive Gospel Sources,* pp. 15-22. New York: Philosophical Library, 1951. C. H. Dodd, in *According to the Scriptures* (New York: Charles Scribner's Sons, 1953), argues not so much for a written collection of Scripture texts as for a system of Old Testament interpretation in all the church, using passages familiar from the first sermons.
2. O. Cullmann, *The Earliest Christian Confessions,* translated by J. K. S. Reid. London: Lutterworth Press, 1949.
3. How much the title was used of Jesus in His earthly life is uncertain. It is used of Him seldom in Mark and in the passages common to Matthew and Luke. In John it is not used of Jesus until Peter makes his great confession of faith, "Lord, to whom shall we go? You have the words of eternal life." (John 6:68.) Only in the last half of John is the title repeatedly used. Perhaps this implies that the title was one which the disciples could not bestow upon Jesus until they had begun to realize something of His true significance.
4. There were many "lords" in the "mystery religions" of the time. The "lord" of such a religion was a divine being who stood in a special relationship to his followers. He was more human and the object of more heartfelt personal worship than the Olympian deities. The belief in these "lords" may have influenced the spread of Christianity in the Roman Empire, but as used in Acts the title "Lord" is not derived from these pagan cults. This is demonstrated by several writers, including Vincent Taylor in *The Names of Jesus,* pp. 38-51. London: Macmillan and Co., Ltd., 1953.
5. This hymn was probably composed in Aramaic. See Ernst Lohmeyer, *Kyrios Jesus,* p. 9. Heidelberg: Carl Winters, 1928.
6. The Hebrew name for God, "Jehovah" or "Jahweh," was translated in the Greek versions of the Old Testament as "Lord." A pious rabbi reading the Hebrew Old Testament would not pronounce the sacred name "Jahweh" but would say "Lord."
7. The Promised Prophet was sometimes regarded as the forerunner of the Messiah rather than as the Messiah Himself. This distinction, however, was not always carefully maintained, as Josephus makes clear. For extended discussion of "The Prophet" as a Messianic title see Franklin W. Young, "Jesus the Prophet: A Re-examination," in *Journal of Biblical Literature,* Vol. LXVIII, Part IV (December 1949), pp. 285-299.

8. "Manual of Discipline" 9:11; and the fragment described by D. Barthélemy and J. T. Milik in *Discoveries in the Judean Desert,* Vol. I, *Qumran Cave I,* page 121. Oxford: The Clarendon Press, 1955.
9. A highly important Old Testament title used of Jesus in Acts is "Servant." (Isaiah 42:19; Acts 3:13.) We postpone discussion of this concept until the next chapter, when we comment on the meaning of the cross.

Chapter 5

Jesus, a Man on Earth

1. Matthew 2:23. This is an example of that new kind of interpretation of the Old Testament which enabled Christians to find Jesus everywhere foretold in the Hebrew Scriptures. See Chapter 4, pp. 50-51.
2. Chapter 4, p. 53.
3. Weiss, *Christ, the Beginnings of Dogma,* p. 43.
4. "It is not the least remarkable feature of the Gospels as historical documents that although they all—even Mark—are written under the influence of a 'high' Christology, yet they all—even John—represent Jesus as a teacher with His school of disciples." C. H. Dodd, in *Mysterium Christi,* p. 53, edited by G. K. A. Bell and D. Adolf Deissmann. New York: Longmans, Green and Co., 1930. Used by permission.
5. Isaiah 61:1-2. Its language is reflected in Acts 10:38; compare Luke 4:18-19.
6. The form critic Martin Dibelius lists these stories in Mark as most clearly betraying by their literary style their first use as sermon illustrations:

The Healing of the Paralytic	Mark 2:1 ff.
The Question of Fasting	Mark 2:18 ff.
The Rubbing of the Ears of Corn	Mark 2:23 ff.
The Healing of the Withered Hand	Mark 3:1 ff.
The Relatives of Jesus	Mark 3:20 ff., 30 ff.
Blessing the Children	Mark 10:13 ff.
The Tribute Money	Mark 12:13 ff.
The Anointing in Bethany	Mark 14:3 ff.

Martin Dibelius, *From Tradition to Gospel,* p. 43; translated from the second edition of *Die Formgeschichte des Evangeliums* by Bertram Lee Woolf. New York: Charles Scribner's Sons, 1935. Used by permission.

7. Acts 2:23; 3:15; 4:10; 5:30; 10:39.
8. J. S. Stewart, *A Man in Christ,* pp. 228-230. New York: Harper & Brothers (n.d.). Used by permission.
9. The Greek word *pais* is translated here as "Son" in the King James Ver-

sion, but the Revised Standard Version is better in translating the word as "Servant" in this context.

10. Isaiah 42; 49; 50; 52; 53; 61; etc. Not all scholars today would regard Isaiah 61 as by the same hand and one with the "Servant poems" of the other chapters. There is no indication, however, that first-century readers would have made this distinction, and Isaiah 61 does have close affinities with the "Servant poems" such as Isaiah 53.
11. It is agreed by most students of the Dead Sea scriptures that they offer no concept parallel to this Christian identification of "Messiah" and "Servant." See T. H. Gaster, *The Dead Sea Scriptures,* p. 19.
12. Mark 1:11 (compare Isaiah 42:1); 8:31; 9:12; 9:31; 10:33; 10:45.
13. The word for "servant" in Philippians is *doulos.* The word in Acts and the Greek translation of Isaiah is *pais.* However, if the Philippians passage was indeed an Aramaic hymn the word in the Aramaic original may have been the same as that used by Isaiah.
14. For additional support for this conclusion read A. E. J. Rawlinson, *The New Testament Doctrine of the Christ,* pp. 238-241. London: Longmans, Green and Co., Ltd., 1926.

Chapter 6

Jesus, the Risen and Exalted One

1. A. E. J. Rawlinson, *The New Testament Doctrine of the Christ,* p. 31.
2. Romans 4:25; 8:11; Galatians 1:1; 2 Corinthians 4:14; 1 Peter 1:21.
3. Examples: 1 Corinthians 15:1-11; Romans 1:1-4. See the appendix of C. H. Dodd's *The Apostolic Preaching and its Developments.*
4. The phrase "the right hand of God" or its equivalent is used in connection with Jesus 17 times in the New Testament in 8 different books. See also the discussion of Psalm 110 in this volume, Chapter 4, pp. 55-56.
5. Paul Wernle, *The Beginnings of Christianity,* Vol. I, pp. 128 ff. Translated by G. A. Bienemann. New York: G. P. Putnam's Sons, 1903.
6. For a development of the "adoptionist" view see the writings of Johannes Weiss, for example: *Christ, the Beginnings of Dogma.*
7. Jackson and Lake rightly point out that Luke's careful recording of such different views indicates that he was probably using several ancient written sources. *The Beginnings of Christianity,* Vol. IV, p. 120.
8. See note 6 above.

Chapter 7

Jesus, a Living and Present Power

1. Westminster Shorter Catechism, answer to question 6; compare the Nicene Creed.
2. Silva New, "The Name, Baptism, and the Laying on of Hands," in Jackson and Lake, *The Beginnings of Christianity,* Vol. V, pp. 124-125.
3. In Galatians 2, Paul assumes that Peter and the other leading preachers of the early church were sympathetic toward this idea. He did not think of "justification by faith" as a new discovery of his own but rather as something implied by all who preached baptism for forgiveness in Jesus' name. His opponents had simply failed to think through to Paul's conclusions the implications of what they themselves preached.
4. Also translated "Prince," or "Pioneer," or "Author," or "Leader." (Greek: *archegos.)* See Chapter 4, pp. 58-59.
5. James Denney, *Jesus and the Gospel,* p. 18. London: Hodder and Stoughton, Ltd., 1908. Used by permission.

Chapter 8

Jesus in the Preaching of Stephen

1. For a critical study of Stephen's address and a history of its interpretation supporting this view see R. J. Knowling, "The Acts of the Apostles," *The Expositor's Bible,* Vol. II, pp. 204-207.
2. In support of this see especially William Manson, *The Epistle to the Hebrews,* p. 37. London: Hodder and Stoughton, Ltd., 1951.
3. Daniel, it is true, seems to identify the Son of man with "the saints of the most high" (Daniel 7:18), but the use of the term in Enoch and in such passages as Matthew 25:31 indicates that in Jesus' day the expected "Son of man" was often thought of as a heavenly individual.
4. "Testament of Benjamin" 9:2, a contemporary Jewish prophecy. We have deleted from the quotation phrases which R. H. Charles regards as later additions by Christians.
5. Philo wrote a few years after Stephen preached. What is suggested here is not that Stephen was dependent upon Philo himself but that Philo illustrates a system of Biblical interpretation through types which was known in Hellenistic Judaism.

CHAPTER 9

JESUS IN THE PREACHING OF PAUL

1. See also 1 Corinthians 1:23; 2 Corinthians 4:5.
2. Maurice Jones lists many parallels between this address and Paul's letter to the Galatians. (The church at Antioch is probably one of those to whom Galatians was written.) Among these parallels are: Israel's history is seen as a preparation for Christ, a "schoolmaster." (Galatians 3:24.) Israel is a son cared for by a Father. (Acts 13:17; Galatians 4:1-7.) The theme of sonship is also applied to Christ. (Acts 13:33; Galatians 4:4.) The concept of "rejection" by God has a place, illustrated by Canaan and Saul in Acts and by Hagar in Galatians. Certain peculiar words are strikingly paralleled: *fulfill, tree, free* or *justify*. Other parallels might be noted. Maurice Jones, *St. Paul the Orator,* pp. 52-58. London: Hodder and Stoughton, Ltd., 1910. Used by permission.
3. R. G. Finch notes three rare verbs in Paul's introduction: *exalted* (Acts 13:17, K.J.V.; Isaiah 1:1-2, A.S.V. margin), *bore* (Acts 13:18; Deuteronomy 1:31), and *gave for an inheritance* (Acts 13:19; Deuteronomy 1:38). The reference to *judges* (Acts 13:20), never mentioned elsewhere in the New Testament, might have been suggested by Isaiah 1:26. Deuteronomy 1 and Isaiah 1:19, passages that fit well in words and meaning as a background for Paul's sermon, were the lectionary readings for a fall sabbath in A.D. 47, just about the time of Paul's visit to Antioch. R. G. Finch, *The Synagogue Lectionary and the New Testament,* p. 87. London: Society for Promoting Christian Knowledge, 1939.
4. F. J. Foakes-Jackson, *The Acts of the Apostles,* p. 118. (Moffatt Commentary Series.) New York: Harper & Brothers (n.d.). Used by permission.
5. Though Paul's survey of the Old Testament history is similar in form to Stephen's there are sharp differences. Paul does not make such use of typology and allegory. And for Paul the Old Testament is the story of God's grace. Stephen emphasizes rather the frustration of hope.
6. The King James Version uses "Son" in Acts 3:13. A better translation here, however, is "Servant."
7. See note 3 above.
8. Here is another example of titles first applied to God's chosen people being now applied to Jesus. For others see Chapter 4 on *Stone,* Chapter 5 on *Servant,* etc.

CHAPTER 10

JESUS IN THE NEW TESTAMENT WRITINGS

1. See Chapter 5, pp. 69-70.

CHAPTER 11

WHAT DO YOU THINK OF THE CHRIST?

1. For example, Harnack writes: "The formation of a correct theory of and about Christ threatens to assume the position of chief importance, and to pervert the majesty and simplicity of the Gospel." This "perversion" he charges to Paul. Adolf Harnack, *What Is Christianity?*, p. 198.
2. Martin Dibelius, *From Tradition to Gospel*, p. 295.
3. From the hymn, "The Head That Once Was Crowned with Thorns," by Thomas Kelly.
4. From the hymn, "Lead On, O King Eternal," by Ernest W. Shurtleff.

Index of Scripture

Index of Subjects